2018

MW00874505

Dear Bill & Virginia

May all Your days be Roses —

Leave the onions in the Kitchen!

Enjoy my second Book ☺

Love,

Donna Puglisi

AuthorHouse™
1663 Liberty Drive
Bloomington, IN 47403
www.authorhouse.com
Phone: 1 (800) 839-8640

Published by AuthorHouse 03/28/2018

ISBN: 978-1-5462-3103-5 (sc)
978-1-5462-3104-2 (e)

Library of Congress Control Number: 2018902475

Print information available on the last page.

Any people depicted in stock imagery provided by Getty Images are models,
and such images are being used for illustrative purposes only.
Certain stock imagery © Getty Images.

This book is printed on acid-free paper.

Because of the dynamic nature of the Internet, any web addresses or links contained in this book may have changed
since publication and may no longer be valid. The views expressed in this work are solely those of the author and do
not necessarily reflect the views of the publisher, and the publisher hereby disclaims any responsibility for them.

authorHOUSE®

Roses

and

Onions

One Layer at a Time

by Donna Puglisi

ILLUSTRATED

by

WILL LILIENTHAL

ABOUT THE ILLUSTRATOR

WILL LILIENTHAL

Will was born in Brooklyn, New York in 1965. He was a Fine Arts major at Norwich Free Academy High School in Norwich, CT, class of 1983.

After high school, he attended the Art Institute of Boston, then followed his heart and moved to Florida in 1986. Presently, he is employed by Brevard County Fire/Rescue as a professional Firefighter/Paramedic for the past 25 years.

"Roses and Onions, One Layer at a Time" is Will's first collaboration on a book as an illustrator. After a 20-year hiatus as an artist, he said, "I give full credit to Donna Puglisi, for encouraging and inspiring me to continue to draw and create."

(Author's Note): There will be many more beautiful books to be published and illustrated by Will. His insight and imagination capture every heartbeat and emotion of my poetry.

Will's other great passion is sailing on his boat, "HAWK". May the waters be calm and the winds blow gently through your sails!

Read the first poem, "Will and Hawk". Welcome aboard!

WILL AND "HAWK"

This is how it came to be,
Fate played her hand with Destiny;
Our story gets better still,
Two "Williams" met, called Bill and Will.
'Sailboat for sale, her name is Hawk',
"Sold!" said Will, "Bill, let's talk."

The "Passing of Sails" is a badge of honor,
It is the sailor's creed;
Hoist the mainsail and the jib,
"Old Salts" are a unique breed.
Strong hands steer straight through waters blue,
Pray calm waters flow with you.
Mother of Winds can change on a whim,
A sailor best know how to swim.
Captain Bill is in the winds as the rainbow spinnaker flies,
The hawk's emblazoned on her sail, kissing clouds and crystal skies.

May Neptune bless Will with fair winds, calm seas,
May dolphins swim by his side;
Let sun and stars shine bright upon him,
May good fortune be his guide.

Just as the hawk flies into setting sun,
The sailboat and captain blend as one;
Will and "Hawk", together be,
Sailing on life's endless sea.

THE POET AND THE ARTIST

Every cloud has dimension,
Every wave has a heart;
The palette is a poet's words,
This is her work of art.

An artist weaves his magic with every loving stroke,
The poet danced around him,
Her rhymes and rhythms spoke.

"Our passions may be different,
But similar are we;
My words fill ears with pleasures,
You paint for all to see."

The artist and the poet,
Just like the moon and sun,
complement each other,
each canvas becoming one.

ALSO BY DONNA PUGLISI

"DIAMONDS IN THE ROUGH"

**"You're the gems that don't glitter,
You're the gems that don't shine;
One day you'll be discovered hidden in the mine."**

DEDICATION

For my loving husband, Fred. You are my patient muse. Thank you for your love and constant encouragement. Most of all, thank you for your laughter!

For my angel mom, Mae. Oh, how I miss you! You are my "ghost writer". I know you're guiding me every step of the way on my exciting life's journey.

For my dad, Frank, the "sports guru". Although you don't really read poetry, you understand me, and that's all that matters.

Thank you, Will Lilienthal, for your artistic talent. You make my book come alive! Not only are you a firefighter/paramedic/hero/friend, but your enthusiasm and imagination constantly inspire me.

These are my precious "layers", my roses and onions!

Donna Puglisi

ROSES AND ONIONS, ONE LAYER AT A TIME

Layer upon layer, we build our lives. Some of us are as big as the Rock of Gibraltar, while others are sand pebbles on a beach.

One layer at a time, one experience at a time. This defines who we are. Peel back those layers like an onion and you will expose the true heart of a man, the core of the human psyche.

Admire a rose's beauty. It has infinite layers of delicate spiraling designs. Each petal is unique, like all of us. My poetry has many layers too. Humor, love, wonder, sadness, elation. Like rings on a tree or a single snowflake, not one of us is the same. We make the earth spin. We are all poetry in perpetual motion.

Without the poet, what a dull gray world this would be. From my opening poem, "Layers":

"Freedom is a state of mind,
Let loose the doves to soar;
Breaking through, reborn again,
It's just one layer more."

Donna Puglisi

ROSES & ONIONS, ONE LAYER at a TIME

CONTENTS
LAYER BY LAYER

LAYER 1:   I CALL IT AS I SEE IT

Layers	1
The Rose And The Onion	2
Once Upon A Rhyme	3
Dance Every Day	4
Stepping Stones	5
The Wish	6
Stepping Up To The Plate	7
One of These Days	8
I'm Alive To Tell About It	9
The Biggest Man	10
Predator	11
The Wall Of Hatred	12
In A Nano Second	13
Running Out Of Road	14
The Deep Pour	15
A Wisp Of A Man	16
The Void And The Veil	17
The Widows Walk	18
Look Through Her Eyes	19
Aged Like Her Wine	20
Walking On Water	21
Silver And Salt	22

One Palm Tree At A time 23
Breaking Through The Walls 24
Desperate 25
Two Snakes 26
The Tea Party 27
On Shaky Ground 28
Little Pig, Little Pig Let Me In 29
A Salmon Swimming Upstream 30
Peace 31
Ivory Towers 32
Clinging To Driftwood 33
Fate And Destiny 34
Sifting Through The Ashes 35
Feel 36
The Fork In The Road 37
The Great Massage 38
Chipping Away At Stone 39
Forgetting To Remember 40
Deep 41
Whisper 42
Guitarist 43
Pearls And Oysters 44
Grasping At Straws 45
Black Widow 46
Moody 47
90 Degrees 48

LAYER 2:   THE NATURAL ORDER OF THINGS

Wading Through The Waters 49
A Whale Of A Tale 50
Looking Through The Eyes Of A Dove 51
Running Barefoot In The Rain 52

November   53
Winter's Woes   54
Loony Tunes   55
A New Day   56
Whistling Winds   57
The Royal Ones   58
Heavy   59
Soft   60
Two Doves On A Rooftop   61
Morning   62
The Beauty Of A Rose   63
Mist On The Water   64
The Perfect Day   65
Dimples On The Lakes   66
Time To Sleep   67
Subtle   68
Icicle   69

LAYER 3:   LAUGHTER, THE BEST MEDICINE

Laughter   70
Cigars Aren't Just For Men   71
The Not-So-Dandy Dandelion   72
A Norman Rockwell Thanksgiving   73
A Polar Bear In Florida   74
For Medicinal Purposes Only   75
Don't Let Your Knees Get In The Way   76
Stuff   77
King Raven   78
Trying To Catch A Gecko   79
If You Can't Cut The Mustard, You Can't Ketchup!   80
Cow Tao   81

Please Don't Burn The Bacon!   82
The Cheese Stands Alone   83
The Nitty Gritty   84
I Just Came By To Borrow A Cup Of Sugar   85
Pretending To Be In Barcelona   86
Welcome To My Twilight Zone   87
Life Is Too Short Not To Have Room Service   88
The House Knows   89
Being Bald   90
Smoked Salmon And Roe   91
Distinguished vs Extinguished   92
Noise   93
Vincent's Ear   94
The Nervous Knee   95
Dirty Old Men   96
Mark Your Balls, Boys   97
Mundane Monday   98

LAYER 4:   ROMANCING THE ROSE

Lover   99
Sexy Blue Eyes   100
I Used To Feel   101
One Summer Day   102
No Claim, No Blame   103
Poison In The Well   104
Almond Eyes   105
The Richest Woman In The World   106
Come To Your Lady In Dreams   107
Spontaneous Combustion   108
While You Can   109
Rainbow   110

Time With You   111
Anchor   112
The Lost Art Of Conversation   113
Seeing Through A Brick Wall   114
If You Can   115
Buried Six Feet Under   116
From Friend To Fiend   117
Daze   118
Illicit Love   119
Worship   120
Holding Hands   121
Tears   122
You'll Make A Hell Of An Angel   123
Pale Blue   124
She Is Love   125

LAYER 5:   OUR HEROES

My Every Day Hero   126
The Thin Blue Line   127
Last Call   128
Wreaths Across America   129
Core   130
Behind The Face   131
Standstill   132
Camouflage   133
Veteran   134

LAYER 6: FAMILY & HOME

Windy	135
The Keys To Happiness	136
My Little Man	137
Delicate	138
My Dad	139
The Old Black Lunch Box	140
My Mom	141
Ghost Writer	142
Roses For Mama	143
A Special Sunday	144
Sarah's Fight	145
A Thanksgiving Prayer	146
I Want To Live In Mayberry	147
Walking With Sophie	148
Hummingbird	149
Olivia In Pigtails	150
Grandpa's Leather Boots	151
Lake's End	152
Home Sweet Home	153
Safe In My Arms	154

LAYER 1:

I CALL IT AS I SEE IT

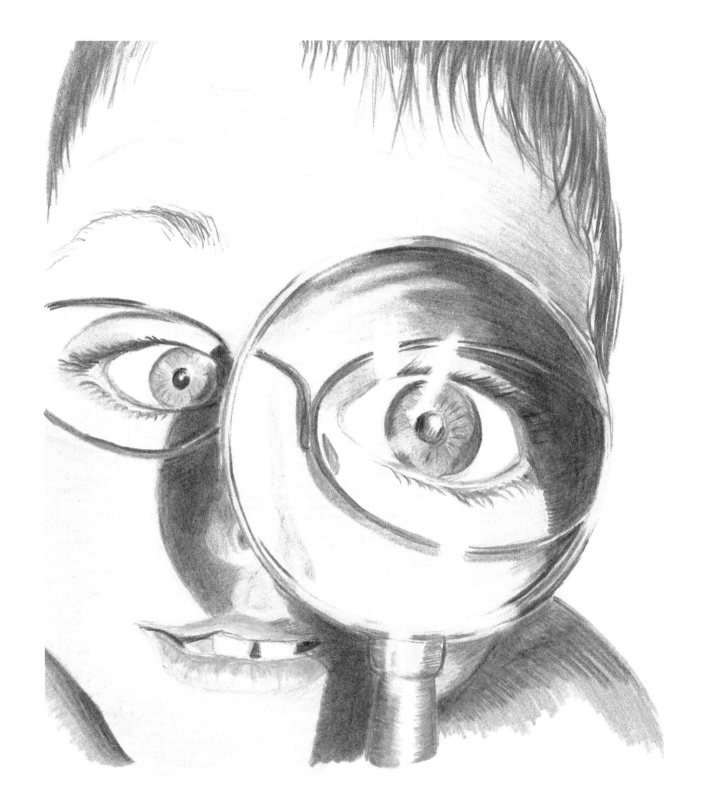

LAYERS

Another layer peeled away,
Another revelation;
Is this cause for panic or a celebration?

Exposing my inner core, like an apple gutted,
Private no more;
I'm out there for all to see,
There is no façade,
Just my honesty.

Dancing on hot coals,
I've grown a calloused skin;
Free from insecurities,
I found my peace within.

Sifting through the rubble one layer at a time,
Unearthing hidden treasures,
I finally hit my prime.

I've risen like a French souffle,
Peacefully I sleep;
I'm no longer the meager scrap at the bottom of the heap.

Freedom is a state of mind,
Let loose the doves to soar!
Breaking through, reborn again,
It's just one layer more.

THE ROSE AND THE ONION

Once the layers are peeled away, the true heart of a man is exposed

An onion was planted next to a rose,
In the garden the two were alone and exposed;
One was a beauty, her scent endearing,
The other, acidic, and very eye-tearing.

The rose bent her lovely stem to the onion,
"We're both the same, you see;
Let's peel back our layers one by one,
and reveal who we really can be!"

The onion was sweating, no match for this rose,
He blushed as he shredded his oniony clothes;
The onion's garments were smooth and round,
His layers fell softly to the ground.

Her pretty red petals dropped one by one,
Down to her core, she faced the onion;
"My, you're a rich one! You smell of the earth,
Mr. Onion, you've shown me just what you're worth;
Layer by layer, your inner core made me love you so much more!"

"And you, dear Rose, don't need a petal
to show your true heart, strength and mettle!"

Once the layers are peeled away, one's soul and spirit shine through,
Whether you're an onion or rose,
True beauty lies deep within you!

ONCE UPON A RHYME

Once upon a rhyme in another time
a musician roamed the streets;
With lyre in hand, a one-man band
sang songs for food to eat.

The poet wrote his rhyming verse
for all to hear his story;
He sang of love, he sang of soldiers
fighting for God and glory.

Farmers laid down plows in fields,
King's armies put away their shields;
All listened to the poet's song,
singing as he strolled along.

Musicians and poets brought joy to life,
Easing burdens of daily strife;
Peasants smiled and danced to their tunes,
Romance blossomed under harvest moons.

Once upon a rhyme in another time,
A poet reigned as king;
Respect and praise in olden days,
To the poet we will sing!

Ballads of love, songs of sorrow,
Live for today for a better tomorrow;
A poet am I till the day I die,
Once Upon a Rhyme!

DANCE EVERY DAY

Dance every day,
Love until your heart bursts.

Cherish the small moments,
They are the biggest ones of all.

STEPPING STONES

One step at a time,
One stone at a time.

Your hand guides me over troubled waters.

Ill winds might blow,
I'll weather the storm;
With steady steps, you lead me to shore,
to my haven, safe and warm.

I have no fear, I have no doubts.

It's just one stepping stone at a time.

THE WISH

I wish I was Peter Pan flying to Never Never Land,
Free to choose my destiny,
Happy as a boy should be.

I have no hair, bound by this chair,
No legs to run and play;
They say I'll beat this cancer and live for another day.

I wish an angel would take me to a far and distant place,
Maybe the Man in the Moon has a plan for me,
As I gaze upon his face.

Each day I try to be strong and brave,
But deep inside I know
My life is short, and in my heart,
to a man I'll never grow.

I wish my parents didn't cry each time they look at me,
Nobody dares to speak the truth out loud,
Soon I'll be a memory.

I wish upon the biggest star twinkling in the night,
One day I'll be that brilliant orb shining ever bright!

Wishes maybe can come true,
and if mine ever do,
Know that in my heart and soul,
I'm forever loving you.

STEPPING UP TO THE PLATE

When it comes down to brass tacks,
Take the bull by the horns;
Put on that jock strap,
Cut a swath through the thorns.

Like a batter and a pitcher,
Don't hesitate,
Anticipate the fast ball;
Just step up to that plate.

Bat a thousand, make a home run,
Being the one in charge isn't that much fun.
When there's no one else to rely on,
Be the one with balls;
Step up to that plate,
Wack the hell out of it!
The coward's the one who stalls.

ONE OF THESE DAYS

"One of these days" never comes
unless you make it happen;
"One of these days" is a promise never kept,
"One of these days" is a coin in a fountain,
On my shoulders you sadly wept.

A young man's dreams and ambitions
once written in stone,
Now find you old, forgotten,
broken and alone.

"One of these days" turns into a lifetime,
Moments of regret;
Procrastinations, bad decisions,
Fortunes lost on a lousy bet.

You can never get those years back,
No matter how hard you try;
"One of these days" finally came due,
A squandered life passed by.

I'M ALIVE TO TELL ABOUT IT

He sat alone and vulnerable,
Revealing a wounded heart;
He bared his soul, naked among friends,
His world was torn apart.

He cried the tears of anguish,
His nightmares were revealed;
One layer at a time exposed,
Like an onion peeled.

"I'm alive to tell about it,
I don't know how or why";
With a quivering mouth,
He fought hard not to cry.

Drowning in a sea of insanity,
He stared into the eyes of death;
Caught up in a whirlpool of madness,
fighting for his life, gasping for breath.

Pulled from black cold waters,
A prisoner no more;
Through the gates that held him once,
He found an open door.
Compassion, love and kindness won his uphill fight,
Renewed, reborn in God's great love,
He finally saw the light.

THE BIGGEST MAN

The Biggest Man in the room had tears in his eyes.
He sat alone, eating his dinner, head bowed,
drowning in his sorrows.

The Biggest Man in the room had the heart of a lion,
Vulnerable in his honesty, with the innocence of a young boy.

Amidst the noise and confusion,
he sat in silence, then turned to me and smiled.

Slowly, with a heavy sigh, he pulled himself up into his wheelchair.
Eyes still wet with tears, The Biggest Man in the room rolled away,
Fading into the crowd,
Insignificant as a shadow,
Invisible as a ghost.

With just one look and a smile,
I loved his beauty.

PREDATOR

Beware of the handsome face,
The laugh, the pat on the back;
The one telling jokes to all the folks,
Be careful,
He's a predator.
The life of the party, everyone's friend,
Sociopath, he tries to blend;
There's a monster lurking behind the mask,
The façade he puts on every day;
He's the guy lusting after children
on the school grounds at play.
That smooth talker is a stalker,
Hanging out in sleazy bars;
Luring women to his lair,
or a quickie behind parked cars.
Liar without a conscience,
Deadly thorns of deceit,
A shadow lurking in back alleys,
Jack the Ripper,
Lethal, discreet.

Sex, lies and videotapes,
Your life is now on file;
What goes on behind closed doors?
He'll kill you with a smile.

PREDATOR

THE WALL OF HATRED

The wall looms high, forbidden,
Between the cracks, hatred is hidden;
It seeps through bricks made of rage,
Black, foreboding, a tormentor's cage.

Hatred stops you from moving forward,
Consuming like a fire;
Only ashes and bits of bone
are left on the funeral pyre.

Break the chains that bind you,
A slave no more, set free;
Blind men shed dead gauzy eyes
so they can finally see.

Love awaits you on the other side,
Hope triumphs in the void;
The wall will fall brick by brick,
until it is destroyed.

IN A NANO SECOND

One day you're at home,
Snug and cozy, everything's rosy;
The next day in the foray your life changes, rearranges.

What the hell happened?

What once was my home, vowing never to roam,
Hoping I would die in bed,
Now it's four walls, a walker, a wheelchair,
Wishing I was dead.

In a nano second, it's all gone,
Memories stripped from the walls,
My life's askew, nothing to do.

What went wrong?

The "Golden Years" aren't so golden,
I'm just a dying sheep in the fold;
Guess I gotta roll like the Stones,
"What a drag it is getting old"!

RUNNING OUT OF ROAD

In younger days, the roads stretched for miles and miles. They seemed endless, eternal, infinite. We never dreamed that one day we would just run out of road.

As kids, we'd walk for miles on the old dirt paths winding in and out of wooded hills. We were on our exciting new adventures, never quite sure where our paths would take us.

The dusty dirt roads soon became highways. New cars traveled across the country, replacing our bare feet and Tom Sawyer dreams. The roads still beckoned us. So many miles to travel!

Faster, faster, life's journeys wrapped around the world like an orb spinning out of control. Soon there were roadblocks.
No Trespassing! Stop! Do Not Enter! Do not! Do not! Do not!

What is it that we forgot?

I reminisce about those slower days, simpler ways. Those old dirt paths. As I get older in my sunset years, I see the end of my wanderlust, unreachable, taunting me just over those formidable looming hills ahead.

I never thought that someday I would just run out of road.

THE DEEP POUR

Just a few ounces more,
Your feet never touch the floor;
Innocent little glass of wine,
sipping slowly as you dine.

I'll have another, if you please,
It goes down quickly with such ease;
Satiated is overrated,
Last call for alcohol;
One more for the road,
I'll leap like a toad,
Hope I don't hit that wall.

Those luscious ruby reds, life dangles on a vine,
The Grapes of Wrath make a path
for that deep pour of overindulging;
Too much of anything is no good,
My eyes are red and bulging.

Another hangover, another lost weekend,
Too many excuses, lose another friend;
Do I dive into shallow waters head-first and hit the rocks?
Save me from myself, dear Lord,
and that wooden box.

The deep blue sea beckons me,
as I sink to ocean's floor;
Drink from the fountain of excess,
Just give me another deep pour.

A WISP OF A MAN

Look at you.

You blend with the bar stool,
One with the chair;
A whisper, a wisp of thin air.

Old man with a hat too big for your head,
Pale as a corpse,
You're the walking dead.
Where do you go when your drinking is done?
Are you alone or do you love someone?

Look at you,
A wisp of a man;
Have another beer,
Drink while you can.
You'd blow away with a summer breeze,
Slide off the chair onto your knees.

As you weave your way through the crowd,
You share your thoughts, talking out loud;
Frail as a rail,
Go home, drink some more;
Wake up with a hangover,
passed out on the floor.

A wisp of a man,
Just a wisp of a man

THE VOID AND THE VEIL

Peering through the misty veil,
They look at you with loving eyes;
They are everywhere,
They are always with you

When you lose a loved one,
When the void is too wide to fill,
look through the eternal veil;
It is shrouded in ethereal gray,
a world between light and dark.

Love is the bridge between life and death.
Love will take you by the hand
on a journey beyond the horizon.
Love will always guide you,
Love is eternal.

THE WIDOWS WALK

One, two, three, four,
Another house for sale;
Another funeral service,
Oh, how they look so pale.

The widows walk around the block,
Where do they go from here?
Estate sale signs are everywhere,
Off to a nursing home, we fear.

They outnumber widowers,
Those old men hanging tough;
Some resilient, set in life,
Some haven't got enough.

Around the block,
It's the widows walk,

Another memory for sale.

LOOK THROUGH HER EYES

The eyes of wisdom,
The eyes of age,
Look through the eyes of this grand old sage.

Every wrinkle on her face
tells a story of time and space;
Haunting stark reality,
Beautiful is her frailty.

Where have you been?
What have you seen?
What knowledge from you can we glean?

A lifetime is a speck of dust,
Succumb to death, finally we must;
Cherish your days on this earth,
It is God's gift from day of birth.

One hundred and six years she wears with pride,
dignity and grace;
Look through the eyes of this old soul,
Look at her beautiful face!

AGED LIKE HER WINE

She was almost 100 years old, aged like the red wine she sipped.

With a smile on her face,
The shrinking violet snuggled in the restaurant booth,
enjoying every drop of wine,
the ruby fountain of youth.

She didn't care about the occasional stare,
She didn't have to hurry;
Aged like her wine, that jewel of the vine,
She was free of stress and worry.

One more glass, her gnarled hand held the fragile stem,
Her daughter hugged her mother tight,
How loving, the two of them.

Wrinkled lips caressed the glass,
Stained with red wine bold;
Savoring each drop, not a care in the world,

After all,
She was almost 100 years old.

WALKING ON WATER

I walk on shimmering moon paths, traversing the sea,
Night's shining stars beckon to me;
I turn water to wine,
Teach disciples to pray,
Cleansing their souls for Judgment Day.
Feed the starving masses on one loaf of bread,
Crucified on the cross, rising from the dead.
But I am just a man.

Born in a stable, earthen floor for my bed,
A heavenly halo crowns my head;
I walk among the lowly poor, make a blind man see;
On this earth, a humble mortal be.

The sins of the world are heavy to bear,
Enemies surround me, into Satan's eyes I stare;
Alone in the desert I sit and pray,
If I were a coward, I could walk away.
I walk on water,
I am the Hope of Mankind;
I endure pain and torture,
This I don't mind.
It's the souls of the lost ones,
Their cries haunting me;
When they touch my robe,
The Son of God they see.

SILVER AND SALT

The stab in the back,
The knife in the heart,
I can't tell you and Judas apart.

Silver coins and salt lay on the table,
Run and hide, dark Judas,
if you're able.

Slithering shadow, black your soul,
Crawling back into your hole;
Betrayer with a silver tongue,
Born a bad seed very young.

A snake like Satan spewing lies,
Evil lurks behind your eyes.

I don't believe a word you say,
They'll haunt your hellish dreams one day;
Two faces when you look at me,

Silver and salt is all I see.

ONE PALM TREE AT A TIME

Step by step, he shuffled along the sidewalk. Today he could walk to
the first palm tree. That was his goal.

One palm tree at a time.

In a week, it would be the second palm tree, then, back to the house.
It seemed like a jungle of palm trees to cover if he could make it
around the block.

He was persistent.

That old heart of his was still beating after the surgery. Shuffle,
shuffle, beat, beat, beat.
Shuffle, shuffle, down the street.

One more palm tree to conquer,

One palm tree at a time

BREAKING THROUGH THE WALLS

Who needs a cape and tights?

You don't have to be a super hero to break through walls,
They're not all concrete and bricks;
Invisible fences can be climbed,
They're not made of wires and sticks.

A boundary's lines and borders, too,
are placed to protect me and you;
Break through walls of fear and hate,
starting with one kind word;
One voice becomes millions strong,
Around the world they're heard.

Super Man is every man,
A hero lies within;
Break through the walls with faith and love,
Only then will change begin.

DESPERATE
The Deep Dark Place

Chip, chip, chip away,
Her world was crumbling day by day;
No pills or meds could numb enough,
Just band aids on a wound;
Too wide her canyon void to fill,
Too deep, too much blood to spill.

Pulled underneath the rip tide,
Drifting far from shore,
Ravenous ravens cried,
"Never more! Never more!"

Rushing waters covered her head,
Praying to God, wishing she was dead.

She was drowning

The last salty gulp,
The last desperate cry for help,
Succumbing to welcoming blackness,
She finally found peace.

TWO SNAKES

Two snakes are we,
Our fangs you cannot see;
One venomous bite, it's over.
There is no hope, no lucky charm,
No pretty four-leaf clover.

Slithering silently on the ground,
You'll never know that we're around;
Don't run for cover, no one can save you,
Voracious, vicious,
Devour you, crave you.

Camouflaged in dark of night,
Wrapped around the tree of Eden;
Don't eat the fruit as the apple falls,
You know it's strictly forbidden.

Two snakes are we,
with hissing, taunting grins,
While you sleep, dear sweet child, your nightmare begins.

THE TEA PARTY

Clink! Clink! Don't hesitate to drink,
Our party's just beginning;
The Queen of Roses wants your head,
The Cheshire Cat is grinning.

Lady Greed rides on her steed
in grand and pompous style;
Lady Pride rides by her side,
with a sly and wicked smile.

Poison runs from jeweled rings,
Don't sip from the silver cup!
Forever dark, the brooding sky,
The sun is never up.

Pull up a chair, but beware,
You won't get out alive;
They dine on weakness, crush a smile,
Only the strong survive.

Welcome to our Tea Party!
Roll out the welcome mat;
The Queen is sitting on her throne,
Grinning like her Cheshire Cat.

ON SHAKY GROUND

I always felt I was straddling the Andreas Fault,
through no fault of my own

Never quite feeling safe,
I stand on shaky ground;
No blanket of security to comfort me
from dangers that abound.

I'm balanced on a tightrope,
One false step, I fall;
Tiptoeing on eggshells, afraid to crack,
I'm Humpty Dumpty on the wall.

Floating through the eye of a tornado,
The calm before the storm,
I want to feel secure and loved,
Wrapped in arms loving and warm.

Free as eagles fly,
With golden wings I'll soar;
Rise above the earthquakes,
On shaky ground no more.

LITTLE PIG, LITTLE PIG LET ME IN

The wolves are at the door,
The vultures are salivating;
It's the smell of decaying flesh,
Another corpse is waiting.

When will he die?
When will we get our money?
The bee hive is empty,
There is no more honey.

When the howling starts,
Beware the full moon;
Dance with the black witch licking her silver spoon.

The pat on the back is the knife that will kill,
Protect the estate,
Protect his last will.

Little pig, little pig,
They're coming to eat you;
Board up the house,
Don't let them defeat you!

A SALMON SWIMMING UPSTREAM

Against all odds,
Against the tide,
The salmon jump, mouths open wide;
The weak are left behind to die,
Only the strong ones pass them by.

Their power is a sexual drive,
Spawning and mating to survive;
Like a salmon swimming upstream,
It's a struggle every day;
Jumping hurdles, dodging bullets,
Lord, give me strength, I pray!

With determination, I set my goals ahead,
Road blocks can be challenging,
So I find new paths instead.

Persistence will eventually pay off in the end,
Take a lesson from the salmon and swim upstream, my friend!

PEACE

Since the birth of mankind, throughout the evolution of civilizations,
Man has been at war. Catacombs dug underground, no room to bury the dead;
no more room to place another tombstone overhead. Remember the crown of
thorns and tread softly on blood-soaked soil. This is the cross we bear, the curse
of war and turmoil.

Looking through the eyes of a dove,
I see a world of peace and love;
I see through blue skies, a brand new day,
I see happy children laugh and play.

There is no bloodshed, there is no war,
There's only peace at heaven's door;
Spirit free, the white bird flies,
Listen to her gentle cries.

Peace reigns like a mighty king,
Through the eyes of a dove, born on a wing.

IVORY TOWERS

Watching the news, I caught my breath,
Disgusted at the violence, horror and death;
Why is it always too late, too late?
Why do we hesitate?

Sitting aloof in our ivory towers,
Heads in the clouds like gods;
Pointing fingers, the stink still lingers,
While politicians look for approving nods.

Eventually towers crack and fall,
The weight of guilt too heavy to bear;
We're swallowed whole, sink into the abyss,
Our cries are everywhere.

Open our hearts to innocence,
as we celebrate mankind's rebirth;
Rebuild our faith in humanity,
Let the children inherit the earth.

CLINGING TO DRIFTWOOD

Feed the hungry children who haven't enough to eat;
They are the little ones starving, begging on the street.

Hollow eyes pleading, can't we see them bleeding?
The weak and the small, God bless them all;
They belong to all of us.

Oh, how it stings, that slap in the face,
We look the other way from the plight of the human race;
The richest nation on earth,
Where freedom got its birth,
Still, our children are starving!

Go to bed hungry, when's my next meal?
Scraps from the garbage,
What can we steal?
Go to school hungry,
What's in your lunch box?
Holes in my shoes, dirty old socks.

Yes, we are the richest nation on earth,
Hurray for democracy, for what it's worth;
Neglect and ignorance can never win,
Our walls are crumbling from within.

FATE AND DESTINY

Stealthy Daughters of Zeus,
entwine us around their dainty fingers;
Gentle arms embrace you,
The perfumed scent of those sisters,
Fate and Destiny, lingers.

Disarming, discreet, you're written in the stars,
As your secrets unfold,
The future is ours;
A twist of fate, mortals are we,
Respect the sisters,
Fate and Destiny.

SIFTING THROUGH THE ASHES

Memories of a lifetime scattered in the wind,
Sifting through the ashes.
Scorched in the fires, loved ones burned,
Our tears fell hard as rain.

Shattered lives, picking up fragments
of a life that once was;
Nothing remains to be reclaimed,
All is lost in the deluge.

Wicked winds taunt and tease,
cursing humanity as we crawl on our knees;
Sifting through the ashes, searching for a prayer,
Hopes and dreams dashed on the rocks,
With dull eyes, in horror we stare.

Peering into the gloom, dark phantoms loom,
hovering, menacing,
disbelieving while we're grieving,
as we continue to sift through the ashes.

FEEL

She was born into a world of silence,
Only touch, the feel of hands on her body,
No sight, no sound,
No words to speak to those around.
The only thing she had was trust,
The only way she could survive was
Feel.

How do you describe a color?
Blue is the sky, green is the grass,
Brilliant hues of rainbow bands,
Feel the rain and sun on your face,
All she could do was trust the hands.

Raging emotions, lost and scared,
Nowhere to hide when your soul is bared;
Drowning in her silent world,
All she could do was feel.

Screaming in her nightmares,
Surrendering to comforting loving arms;
Fingers groping in the coldness of black,
Trust the hands, trust the hands.

She gave the world her light from within;
With strength and courage, the power of love
overcomes all adversity.

Her name was Helen

THE FORK IN THE ROAD

It wasn't a spoon, it wasn't a knife;
It was a fork in the road,
My decision in life.

Should I go left or should I go right?
Throw in the towel or put up a fight?
That fork in the road has a two-pronged sting,
I could end up a winner or lose everything.

"Follow the yellow brick road" in the lovely land of Oz,
Dorothy danced in her ruby shoes,
right into the witch's jaws.
There is no Emerald City shining like a jewel,
No Tin Man, Lion or Scarecrow with hay for brains, no fool.

My compass is my heart,
My path is destiny;
The fork in the road is no obstacle for anyone, but me.
Life is mine to live as I choose,
Walking barefoot or in ruby shoes;
That fork in the road is just a test for me to do what I think best.

Whatever path I choose to follow,
Steadfast is my course;
I'll make decisions bad and good, without regret or remorse.
Confident, I accept my fate, swimming with the tide,
I'll see the horizon, the sun will shine,
And doors will open wide!

THE GREAT MASSAGE

Heal the heart,
Heal the soul,
Listen to the birds in the early morning's light,
Breathe as one.

Clear your mind of all the cobwebs,
Erase negative thoughts,
Concentrate on the beauty around you.

This is

The Great Massage

CHIPPING AWAY AT STONE

They sit like jagged blocks of marble,
Waiting for the gentle hand
to chisel away the layers of stone and sand.

Each one is an angel waiting to fly,
To be released with a kind word,
a loving touch to heal when they cry.
On the wings of a prayer,
Sparks of hope can turn into a flame,
The Phoenix will burn.

Renewed again, the soul reborn,
Slowly chipping away at stone.

Like a butterfly emerging from sleep,
Awake the dreamer, no more to weep;
Stop the silent flow of tears,
Calm the tidal wave of fears.

What wonders unfold when stories are told,
Listen to what they say;
Wisdom of ages speak through these sages,
as memories slowly slip away.

The Master Artist is the Creator,
Supreme Sculptor, divine above;
The Great Equalizer for all men
Is the miracle of Love.

FORGETTING TO REMEMBER

What was it I was going to say?
I should have made a list, anyway;
Little notes I stick on the fridge to jog my memory,
What day of the week is it?
Oh yeah,
I forgot to remember.

It only gets worse with age, they say,
I'm not looking forward to that day;
Wandering from room to room
only adds to my impending doom.

What happens when I wander too far,
forgetting where I parked my car?
Who will help me when my brain cells die?
Huddled in a corner, like a child I cry.

If I look in your eyes, don't know who you are,
Be gentle with me, love,
I just
Forgot to remember

DEEP

Thick with sleep, I lay my head on my cloud of dreams,
Body heavy, I cannot move, as if anchored to my bed;
The only difference between me and a corpse
are my shallow breaths.
I sleep like the dead.

Should I die in my sleep, I go without a fight,
never awakening to a new day,
I fade from sight.

Night cradles me in her blanket of darkness,
tiptoeing into my room,
She is the Keeper of Dreams,
Will I scream tonight
in my nightmarish gloom
or fly with angels?

WHISPER

Whisper, whisper in my ear,
What do you want to say, my dear?
Tell me truths or tell me lies,
Who do you love? Who do you despise?

What horrible things have you done?
Did you wrong or harm someone?
Whisper, whisper in my ear,
Your secret's safe with me, I fear.

I bear the weight of conscience bared,
In me confide, your soul you shared;
I am the keeper, lock and key,
Whisper, whisper, you belong to me.

GUITARIST

Seduce me with your magic fingers,
as Segovia cries on your strings;
Make me weep and swoon
as I listen to your tune;
You are the dancer on the guitar.

Transport me to other worlds,
flying on a song;
Sweet strains flow like tears,
glistening like dew after a summer storm.
Blending as one, she is your Lady.

Happy is my heart,
Full is my soul;
My spirit soars with each sweet note
you so lovingly stroke.

PEARLS AND OYSTERS

Some people are pearls, the jewels in the oyster,
The prize, the hidden treasure;
Some people are oysters, slippery and slimy,
The ocean's decadent pleasure.

Hard to swallow, in sand they wallow,
A pirate's gold of the sea;
The ugly child who rarely smiled,
Not a shining beauty is she.

Which one is the coveted gem, desired?
The tiny pearl in its bed

Or

That gray sloppy slider looking half dead?

GRASPING AT STRAWS

Trying to reach our elusive dreams,
Lofty hopes, ambitious schemes,
Catching butterflies in a net,
racing like the wings of a hummingbird;
We're always seeking that gold at the end of a shimmering rainbow,
but never quite grabbing hold of those
colored gems, quickly dissolving into nothingness.

Grasping at straws,
breaking all the laws, hanging by a thread.
Still we scratch and claw,
praying to the gods on Olympian thrones,
tossing us scraps and discarded bones.

A roulette wheel spinning a fortune
is a greedy man's demise;
Disaster's just around the bend,
Avoid her if you're wise.

A fool's errand, scaling a mountain to reach the top,
Bowing to the Dalai Lama, egos bathe in all the drama.

Power, greed, let it bleed,
We're all just grasping at those damn straws.

BLACK WIDOW

Enticing men to her lacy den,
She spins her web of lies;
Seductive, elusive,
Innocence her disguise.

Venom flows through the fangs
Of those bent on revenge and hate;
The poisonous bite in a deadly fight
served cold on her dinner plate.

Black widow, you sleep in embracing arms,
Weaving your femme fatale magic;
No man can resist your charms,
The outcome predictably tragic.

Black widow, hidden behind your veil,
your victim struggles with a mournful wail;
Delivering that deadly bite,
you disappear in the gloom of night.

Invisible behind your silky wall,
thinking you can fool them all,
you're still a spider, black your heart,
destroying men, lives torn apart.

One day you'll be the helpless prey,
devoured by another;
Every wicked thought and deed
will be his to smother.

MOODY

She was like a black cloud,
ready to burst in a storm.

Her mood was dark, brooding,
hanging gray all day.
When the rain fell,
it fell hard.

Then the sun came out and dried her tears,
She was glowing and warm,
basking in her happiness.

The ground beneath her swallowed her deluge,
ready for her next brewing storm,
because she was so damn

Moody.

90 DEGREES

Bending over, I see the ground,
I can't stand straight or look around;
I'm 90 degrees, a perfect right angle,
My spine is twisted,
My head I dangle.

My friends are every blade of grass,
roots or budding flower;
With my bent and lowly gaze,
I study them by the hour.

I pray one day when I am free
of body's pain and misery,
to be a bird, take wing and fly,
so I can see the world from high!

LAYER 2:

THE NATURAL ORDER OF THINGS

SERENITY

The peaceful sound
of
nothingness

The quiet
of
being

Beauty
in
simplicity

Wrapped
in
Serenity

This is the Natural Order of Things

WADING THROUGH THE WATERS

Each step I take through shallow waters
brings me closer to the meaning of
life's journey.

Unsteady at first, I find a foothold,
sinking into sand;
Slowly I wade through the ebb and flow,
as tiny ripples lap at my ankles.

I walk on beaches drenched in sunshine and salt,
gazing on the horizon ablaze in heaven's hues,
a palette of gold, pink and red.

God has blessed us as we wade through waters,
calm or turbulent;
There is always a rainbow to cling to,
a moon to sing to,
a sun to greet us each morning.

My faith runs deeper than all the oceans,
finding the real meaning of life,

LOVE

A WHALE OF A TALE

On the rocky shores of New England,
The waves crashed with a thunder;
Skies were thick with black stormy clouds,
The ocean churned down under.

Restless were her sea children,
feeling nature's wrath;
The Dance of Whales began
as white foam beat a watery path.

Up and down they splashed
with tumultuous beastly strength;
The mighty whales slapped down their tails,
boasting of their formidable length.

No fisherman dared to interfere,
No man would think of coming near;
They are the Kings of the Briny Sea,
Poseidon's army of behemoths be.

Respect these mighty masters,
Pure beauty to behold;
Ancient relics of centuries past,
Stuff of myths and legends told!

LOOKING THROUGH THE EYES OF A DOVE

I am the spirit of peace and tranquility;
On my wings fly the hopes and dreams of mankind.

I offer the olive branch

Soft, soothing, I am the symbol of love,
quelling the tensions of war and hatred.

I am the Dove,
God's messenger

Calming the constant churning tempests of men,
I am always watching, always protecting.

Listen to my sweet song of spiritual healing.
God's love will be revealed, only if you

Look through the eyes of a Dove

RUNNING BAREFOOT IN THE RAIN

Ditch the shoes, toss them aside,
Run barefoot in the rain!

Oh, that glorious freedom!
Sweet abandon and pleasure,
Running barefoot in the rain.

Feet sinking in the wet grass,
Toes squishing in mud,
Laughing and feeling insane!

To be a child, innocent and wild,
Not a care if they stare with side-glances;
I'm running barefoot in the rain,
Because that's how an angel dances.

NOVEMBER

November exhales her chilly breath,
blowing hard, a prelude to December's icy grip;
Teasingly, she blends with fall's sunshine and warmth,
then turns her cheek away,
not to be kissed by summer's romantic
days or autumn's glowing colors.

Full of promise, November whispers
through corn fields, those sleeping children in their beds
of dry husks;
November's winds blow across the land,
scattering leaves, making way for
December's snowy blanket.

Harvests of gold, plates full of holiday cheer,
She smiles on families gathered together
celebrating her bounty and grace.

Queen of Thanksgiving and love,
November exits for winter's frigid smile,
Dressed in a gown of ice and snow.

WINTER'S WOES

Winter sticks out her tongue
and dares Spring to enter;
Icy is her breath!
She's not willing to succumb,
Spring's rebirth is her death.

Frosty fingers, frozen toes,
A mournful song is Winter's woes;
Grab on to Lady Spring's sweet hand,
as icy sister takes her stand.
One more blizzard's up her sleeve,
Stubborn Winter will not leave.

As is God's plan, each season has her time,
Mother Nature's daughters dance
to the poet's song and rhyme.
Each one has her place, each a different face.

Go to sleep, rebellious child,
God gave you life, on you He smiled;
Frigid sister dressed in white,
Say goodbye to Winter's bite.

LOONY TUNES

Lady loon shrieks like a screaming woman,
Shattering the peaceful silence of morning;
She is the crash of breaking glass,
Her cries cut a jagged wound
in the delicate flesh of dawn's fragile face.
Please stop the bleeding!

Swooning loon, banshee of the lake,
Be considerate, for goodness sake!
You scare the fish, birds fly away,
With your screeching, what are you trying to say?

Is that noise orgasmic pleasure?
Your decibels are hard to measure;
High pitched screams bounce off the water,
You sound as if you're going off to slaughter.

Deafening, you'll wake the dead,
Make a sane man lose his head;
Crazy as a loon, they say,
Leave us in peace and fly away!

A NEW DAY

In the early morning hours of dawn,
a soft breeze playfully tickles feathered palms,
kissing each frond, awakening each to a new morning.

So peaceful is Lady Lake's mood,
not a ripple, as she yawns sleepily,
greeting daybreak.

Silence

Not a soul awakens to disrupt the calm;
Only the white ibis skims the water,
gracefully landing on the edge of a grassy knoll,
wading at the lake's end.

As night slowly departs,
giving way to morning's light,
Pink and gold clouds paint the sky.

God's palette of colors blesses us
with His brand new day.

WHISTLING WINDS

Moving in thin ghostly sheets
across the lake, the water flowed with
the whistling winds.

In and out, she changed directions, as if
teasing and chasing her own rippled tail.

Wild whispers among the trees shattered
the peaceful Sunday afternoon.
"Sylvia", the silver palm tree, waved her
rigid fans, clattering like a Flamenco dancer's *castanets.*

She gracefully stretched her silver fingers to the sky,
trying to catch the fleeting clouds.
I love this day! It reminds me of my own restless spirit.

If I was a phantom riding on the wings of winds,
I would sing through the trees,
in perfect harmony.

THE ROYAL ONES

A crown of fronds you proudly wear,
Like long, flowing locks of untamed hair.

Nature smiled as she blessed her child,
A symbol of sun and sand;
Stretching with ease, these royal trees
Reign supreme across the land.

They are The Royal Ones,
Ageless, wise old sages;
If they could speak, what would they say
as time slowly turns her pages?

HEAVY

Morning lay heavy, barely breathing,
Even the lake stood still;
Not a bird sang its song,
Not a duck swam along,
Not a sign of a fin or a gill.

A lazy breeze sighed wearily,
She was no playful child;
She succumbed to hanging gray clouds,
Flowers lay limp, drenched in morning's mist,
Dressed in their dewy shrouds.

SOFT

Softly, peacefully, the morning rains
lightly, pitting the lake with barely a sound;
Sunday has arrived,
weeping gently in the early hours,
giving way to her sunny sister.

Dark clouds dissipate as she
breaks the gloom with her warming smile;
Softly she enters, tiptoeing cautiously,
So as not to interrupt the breathless silence.

TWO DOVES ON A ROOFTOP

Cooing together, songs of love,
Two doves on a rooftop
sang high above.

Distant from the noisy day,
Two doves cuddled close,
in a place far away.

Are we doves cooing on a roof?
To the world outside, we may seem aloof;
Locked in a trance, eyes for no one else,
Lucky am I, for it's me he loves;
Yes, we are those singing birds,
Two cooing doves.

MORNING

The sky hung gray and cold,
as soft whispers of rain fell on the thirsty
winter brown coat of grass,
remnants of summer,
waiting to breathe warm and green once more.

I listen to nature's conversations,
Aware of her changing moods;
She speaks through the song of a bird,
Dancing as ripples in a lake;
Whistling winds sing her mournful cries,
swiftly changing to teasing laughter on a sunny day.

Morning is a wistful lady,
Her life is short, as she reluctantly relents,
gracefully exiting for a new day to enter.

THE BEAUTY OF A ROSE

A spiraling kiss of delicate design,
Each petal perfect, intricately fine;
Sweet perfumes, unique to each one,
blessed by God's golden rays of sun.

A life too short when cut away,
Will blossom new another day;
If I could choose which flower to be,
admired and loved for all to see,
I'd be a rose, a beauty queen,
exquisite, petals red;
Sparkling like a ruby gem
in my earthly bed.

MIST ON THE WATER

Steaming the cold lake's shallow waters,
Sheets of mist creep slowly over the glassy surface.
Gray fingers stroke her face, barely touching, with a canvas of ghostly white.

Not a ripple emerges under the gauzy blanket, as if sleeping in a trance.

Mist on the water. Misty are my eyes. I never tire of nature's surprise!

Frost hugs the grass, remnants of night's cold breath linger
as morning's sun smiles and melts her to dewy tears.

THE PERFECT DAY

It was a perfect day,
Pure, bright, perfect in every way;
Light blue, the sky, clear and dry;
Powder puff clouds chased by the breeze,
Not a whimper, a cough,
Not even a sneeze!

DaVinci couldn't paint this perfection,
Beauty abundant in every direction;
My head was a swivel whenever I turned,
If this is life's lesson,
There's one thing I've learned.

Just look around you,
There's so much to see!
It was a perfect day,
Lucky, lucky me!

DIMPLES ON THE LAKES

Pitter patter, pitter patter,
Light conversation, rain's quiet chatter;
Gently, she blows kisses on the lakes,
Sleepy Sunday slowly awakes.

Dimples in the water,
Dimples in my smile,
Cozy in my Sunday robe,
Easy calm, my style.

Pitter patter, now lively chatter,
Raindrops quench their thirst;
Weeping, Sunday's heavenly tears bless her children first.

Warming sun will dry them all,
Caressed with fiery golds;
What will Sunday grace us with as her day unfolds?

TIME TO SLEEP

Sleep, my darlings,
You've earned your rest;
All summer long you looked your best.
Green your color, emeralds bright,
Warm breezes kissed by golden sunlight.

Time to sleep in autumn's embrace,
Dying with your dance of grace;
Now you dress in sparkling reds,
snuggling in your earthly beds.

Soon adorned by ice and snow,
Crowned with frost from head to toe;
Bare your branches, arms of white,
Sleep and dream rebirth tonight.

Spring will wake you,
New life will grow;
Ice will thaw, brooks will flow.
So is nature's dance of seasons,
Old gives way to new;
We are one in God's great plan,
We are His children too.

My eyes are heavy with old age,
Loving memories I keep;
It's time to take His holy hand,
It is my time now to sleep.

SUBTLE

Subtle is the breath of a fresh morning breeze,
Dancing lightly on the lake,
a delicate ballerina barely skimming the water.

With a whisper she can kiss the petals of a rose
like a lover.

Subtle, sexy,
Just the way you look at me.

ICICLE

I was born from the cold and water,
Frozen in mid birth;
I hang with winter's breath,
an icicle on this earth.

My time is short,
I dazzle in frigid cloak of white;
Sparkling in the morning sun,
melting in its light.

Dangling precariously,
Held with icy fingers,
Dangerous like a dagger, if my cold heart lingers.

I break into pieces,
Shattered glass and mirror;
An Icicle,
Two sides have I;
One to love and fear.

LAYER 3:

LAUGHTER, THE BEST MEDICINE!

LAUGHTER

What sweet perfume is laughter!
She hangs in the air, suspended there,
Refreshing as rain on a steamy day,
innocent like a child at play.
She has wings, flirtatious nymph,
Happy giggles on a first date;
Running naked, skinny dipping,
a decadent dessert on a plate.

Romancing the moon on a summer night,
The smell of jasmine in the air;
Her smile is a lingering kiss,
Smoldering lovemaking without a care.
Spontaneous eruption, a volcano,
Molten lava laughter;
Rhythmic, rolling, rocking,
spewing from every rafter.

Raucous, she's the sun, the moon,
Bawdy wench of the sea;
Her laughter can make a pirate swoon,
Reigning queen, is she!
Tidal wave, she rushes in,
Untamed, she's running wild;
Blessed Daughter, Pure Love was born,
God blessed us when He smiled!

CIGARS AREN'T JUST FOR MEN

Damn, I wish I had a cigar right now! I feel a rush of testosterone coming on.

Puffing on a cigar, legs crossed,
I know what a man feels like;
No need for balls or other parts,
Don't belch, scratch or sneak in farts.

Cigars aren't just for men,
Havanas feel good between my fingers;
Clouds of smoke hang in the air,
Stale morning stench still lingers.

A glass of cognac by my side,
Blowing smoke rings I do with pride;
Wisps of "O's" are in the air,
as I lean back in my easy chair.

Cigars aren't just for men, you see,
Those brown stogies were meant for me;
What a feeling of feminine power,
Hell, I light one up every hour.

My fingers might be slightly stained,
My teeth a little yellow;
But you can bet one thing for sure,
I rival any fellow!

THE NOT-SO-DANDY DANDELION

I am a dandelion,
not a flower, but a weed;
I am carried by the wind,
not planted like a seed.

No man intended to populate
his manicured green lawn
with the likes of me, annoying rogue,
I am the devil's spawn!

I can't compete with lilacs
Or the beauty of a rose;
You cut me down or spray me
with Home Depot's "weed-free" hose.

I start out bright and sunny,
A cheery little fellow;
I put on a happy face,
with petals brilliant yellow.

When I turn gray and fuzzy,
Tiny seeds I populate
across the lawns for other spawns,
awaiting a similar fate.

Yes, I'm no dandy dandelion,
I'll never win an award;
I guess I'll just resign myself
to be a weed abhorred!

A NORMAN ROCKWELL THANKSGIVING

I used to spend hours just studying Norman Rockwell's
painting of the happy family gathered around the Thanksgiving table.
I wanted us to be that perfect family!

I vowed to make this Thanksgiving dinner
a Norman Rockwell trophy winner!
Wearing my very best holiday smile,
I frantically raced down every aisle.

Butterball turkeys were stocked sky high,
I loaded my cart, topped with pumpkin pie;
Boxes of stuffing were there for the taking,
No slaving over a hot stove baking!
Pushing through people to get out of the store,
I thought of Norman Rockwell once more;
He should have painted our family, instead,
Delusions of grandeur danced in my head!
The day of reckoning finally came,
I think I was the one to blame;
The dog devoured the pumpkin pie,
My biscuits were hockey pucks,
The turkey was dry.
Mashed potatoes and yams were sticky,
Even the stuffing turned out icky!
Then, I looked at my family, laughing and happy,
In the end, was it worth all the fuss?
It was a perfect Thanksgiving after all,
I think Norman would be proud of us!

A POLAR BEAR IN FLORIDA

Here I am, bundled up,
Leather jacket and all;
I look like an autumn leaf in the harvest fall.

Everyone else is showing skin,
My Northern Lights are wearing thin;
High heel boots up to my knees,
Excuse me while I cough and sneeze.

Flip flops, tank tops, show it all,
Goose bumps make my thin skin crawl;
I'm out of place, but I don't care,
Florida's got a polar bear!

FOR MEDICINAL PURPOSES ONLY

In the "still" of the night shines a copper pot bright,
Moonshiners concoct their brew;
150 proof, there is no roof,
In the woods they mix their stew.
Bottles with no labels sit on kitchen tables,
The housewife drinks her dinner, drunk and lonely;
Have a nip, another sip,
It's for "medicinal purposes only".
Revenuers try to flush the moonshiners from their lair,
Locked and loaded, they'll shoot to kill,
Rum runners best beware;
Grandma's sitting on the porch in her rocking chair,
Don't take that bottle from her hands,
She'll bite you, don't you dare!
"For medicinal purposes only",
Put the warning on the bottle;
If you drink enough jet fuel,
You'll be hauling ass full throttle!
Another after dinner drink, put the kids to bed;
The moonshiner is out tonight,
Tax men want him dead.
Under cover in the woods, the copper pot is churning;
Stack the wood, light the fire,
Keep that poison burning;
She sits at home alone at night, drinking to forget,
Churn, churn, churn, burn, burn, burn,
The moonshiner ain't dead yet!

DON'T LET YOUR KNEES GET IN THE WAY

They're your "wheels!
Knee surgery eventually heals;
I never thought when I was young,
my joints would be wet laundry ready to be hung
on sagging clotheslines with aches and pains,
Eventually, I'll remove those stains!

Too many miles to travel,
Don't let your tendons wither and unravel;
I wish I had that lubrication,
just to climb Mt. Everest on my next vacation.

Please, please, give me a new pair of knees,
I'm crawling on the floor;
This nagging pain drives me insane,
I can't take one minute more!

Bone on bone, knee pads don't help,
I can't even stand;
No stairs for me, it's misery,
I need a helping hand.

On this sad note I bid adieu,
Before it's too late, I'm warning you,
Don't let your knees get in the way,
Have that surgery today!

STUFF

Why is letting go so hard?
The more stuff we have,
The more stuff we need to toss,

Eventually.

Until the day of that dreaded departure
from the cluttered garage and the over-crowded closets,

We hoard more stuff.

We attach ourselves to possessions,
bonding over the years,
like good friends.

Sooner or later, we must go our separate ways,
Say goodbye to those dear old buddies,

Our Stuff

KING RAVEN

Black bird, syfy weird as Wes Craven,
Bold, brash, he was known as "King Raven".

Chief of Thieves, strutting head honcho,
If he could, he'd wear a sombrero and poncho;
Screeching to the top of feathered lungs,
Poe would have torn him apart;
Stuffed and mounted on the wall,
Haunted by his "Telltale Heart".

No crumbs for him,
He eats it whole;
King Raven even steals the bowl!
Out-squawking his strongest rival,
King Raven fights for his survival.

No other birds dare interfere,
Might lose a leg or wing;
He's become a legend here,
We crown you "Raven King"!

TRYING TO CATCH A GECKO

Chasing dreams is like trying to catch a gecko;
Bouncing back on canyon walls,
a taunting hollow echo.

My hopes ride on a hummingbird's wings,
whirring in mid-air;
scattering like pearls torn from my neck,
Geckos everywhere!

Hiding in a corner, the shadow of Peter Pan,
slithering between a hairline crack,
Catch me if you can.

Looking in the mirror, haunted eyes I see;
Who's that person staring back?
Is it really me?
I'm water flowing down the drain,
a ripple in a pool,
the student in detention hall staying after school.

Always just within my grasp,
I reach for that brass ring;
I'm trying to catch a gecko,
But I can't catch anything!

IF YOU CAN'T CUT THE MUSTARD, YOU CAN'T KETCHUP!

I'm always the crazy nut in the peanut gallery!

Popcorn, hot dogs, hot buns too,
It's not fun without a brew;
Football, baseball, any game,
I'm a fanatic and my dad's to blame!

On all "fours" by the TV set he curses like a sailor;
I learned new words, four-letter trash,
We should have lived in a trailer!

My blood pressure soars as my team finally scores,
Sweat pours from my brow;
Good ol' dad jumps up and down,
Screaming at the referees now!
"If you can't cut the mustard, you can't ketchup!"
That was his favorite saying;
Mom slams the door in the other room,
My God, I think she's praying!

I admit, I'm over the edge when it comes to sports,
If my team loses, I'll mope for days,
I'm really out of sorts!

The cure for maniacs like me and sports nuts like my papa,
Is just to sit our asses down,
and watch a damn soap opera!

COW TAO

There once was a Chinese cow
Who they called "Cow Tao";
She was admired by everyone,
Even Chairman Mao!
Cow Tao didn't bow to anyone,
She behaved more like a bull;
She wouldn't let the farmer near her udders, very full.
Don't "kowtow" to anyone, don't grovel or show you're weak;
That's how the saying started,
Although we know cows don't speak.
They can "moo" till the cows come home,
But Cow Tao was stubborn and didn't roam.
She stayed put in the farmer's field,
No prodding could ever make her yield;
One day Cow Tao just exploded,
Her udders burst, fully loaded;
The village people jumped for joy,
Fresh meat on every plate;
Sirloin burgers for barbeques,
Time to celebrate!
There's a lesson to be learned,
This advice is "udderly" sound;
Are you the coveted filet mignon
Or the lowly lump of ground round?
Sometimes you have to go with the flow,
Bend or even bow;
Don't end up in little pieces,
Like our beefy friend, "Cow Tao"!

PLEASE DON'T BURN THE BACON!

Grits and eggs for Sunday brunch,
What was breakfast now is lunch;
Ah! That aroma! Whatcha makin'?
Whatever you do,
Don't burn the bacon!

Respect those greasy bacon strips,
Handle them with pride;
Down the hatch, make another batch,
Our mouths are open wide.

French toast tastes awful without a pancake or waffle
drowning in syrup and butter;
The star of the show, is pork belly below,
Crispy bacon just makes my heart flutter!

Hash browns can be crispy,
Martinis stirred, not shaken,
But for heaven's sake,
Don't make the mistake
of burning my morning bacon!

THE CHEESE STANDS ALONE

I never imagined in a million years that I'd be dancing naked in my
family's living room,

Solo

No audience but the empty walls, echoes of memories in the halls.

We need new blood.
I am the Watcher,
The Keeper.
The Midnight Sleeper.

Oh, how the old house groans!
The cheese is moldy and it's beginning to stink,
Rotting pipes, a backed up sink.

This Limburger has to go,

And the cheese stands alone

THE NITTY GRITTY

There's a well-known place in the heart of the city,
It goes by the name of "The Nitty Gritty";
Men go there where the gals are pretty,
Way downtown at "The Nitty Gritty".

Sounds like a strip club, someplace sleazy,
Booze flows fast and the women easy;
It's just a bar to have some fun,
Blow off steam, know everyone.

Darts and pool, dice on the table,
Tequila shots all night, if you're able;
Closing time is 2AM, last call for alcohol,
Sloppy kisses, groping hands,
Girls up against the wall.

What a shame you can't remember in the morning light,
Did you pay your bar tab or get into a fight?
Spent your paycheck, every dime,
Blacked out, Did you have a good time?

Next week you'll just be back for more,
Isn't it a pity?
Forget the mortgage and the rent,
We're going to "The Nitty Gritty"!

I JUST CAME BY TO BORROW A CUP OF SUGAR

Really? A cup of sugar?!
There's a supermarket next door;
Your gossiping tongue annoys me,
I can't stand you anymore.

I'll gladly send you on your way,
Loan you money so you can pay
for that bag of sugar you seem to lack,
Anything, so you won't come back!

What's next? Two shakers of pepper and salt?
If your pantry's empty,
It's not my fault!

May I suggest you do more shopping,
instead of slumming and sleazy bar hopping;
Excuses just don't mean a thing when you're begging on your knees;
I never want to hear you say,

"Can I borrow some sugar, please?"

PRETENDING TO BE IN BARCELONA

I'm sitting in an outdoor café
Imagining a mountain view;
Pretending I'm in Barcelona,
drinking a glass of wine or two.

Sangria flows like water,
Tapas bars await;
Dishes of paella pass me by,
Dinner's after eight.

I could be anywhere now,
Venice, Paris, even Moscow;
But I'll take Barcelona any day,
dreaming all my days away.

When I leave my fantasy,
I face stark reality;
Sipping latte at Starbucks,
Guess Barcelona's not to be!

WELCOME TO MY TWILIGHT ZONE

Surreal. This is how I feel. Spiraling frantically out of control,
I'm Alice in Wonderland;
There is no white rabbit to pour me some tea,
No Mad Hatter to lend a hand.

I'm Dali's melting nightmare,
Rod Serling's demented smile;
Trapped in my private Twilight Zone,
Walking that crooked mile.
Wrapped in a fantasy, twisted and bent,
Reality is just an illusion;
How do I escape this hellish cycle
of out-of-control confusion?
Welcome to my Twilight Zone,
A dimension in outer space;
Nothing is as it should be,
I'm askew and out of place.
Picasso's warped perception,
My reflection in a mirror I see;
Three eyes set back in my forehead,
Who can this person be?
Maybe I should skip the booze,
Stop smoking for a week;
I fear if I don't change my ways,
I'll be a circus freak.

Stay tuned. Don't change that channel.

LIFE IS TOO SHORT NOT TO HAVE ROOM SERVICE

Ring that bell,
Hire a cabana boy,
Life is too short not to have room service.

Order filet mignon, caviar,
A big ol' bucket of champagne.
"Check-out" is soon enough,
Stay a while longer.

Hit the sauna and hot tub,
Enjoy a really sexy massage.
Drink margaritas by the pool.

Ding! Ding! Ding!
Ring that damn bell.
Sooner or later, it's either heaven or hell.
Drink from the fountain of youth,
Enjoy every drop.
Life's eternal clock will never stop.

Room service in your silk PJ's,
Snuggle in your satin bed.
Eventually, it's "Check-Out Time",
Another guest is dead.

THE HOUSE KNOWS

She's a bitch.
She knows when she's being abandoned.
Like a jilted lover, she'll get even with you somehow.

The water heater's first to go,
Smoke alarms beep at 3 AM;
Pipes will burst,
Doors will slam,

She's really pissed.

Groan, creak, a wail, a moan,
She'll never ever leave you alone;
Bricks and plaster,
She's the Master,
She'll shut you in and out;
Basement's flooded in the storm,
Sump pump's a water spout!

The "For Sale" sign flies through the air,
Run for cover, buyer beware;
Yes, the house knows and she won't behave,
She'll send you to an early grave!

BEING BALD

What a blessing to be bald! No hair blowing in the wind,
No stray strands to plaster in place,
No blow dryer detangling that wild mop on top!

It seems being bald is "in",
The chrome dome is admired;
We crave to shave from top to bottom,
Hairless is desired.

I look like a plucked chicken,
Perdue's trophy bird;
Not a hair on my chinny chin chin,
Pubic hair is so absurd!

What happened to the good old days before bikini wax?
Now I strip each curly hair, buffing to the max!
Don't want to look like Kojak,
Scalp gleaming in the sun;
I think I'll grow my mane waist-length,
Flat-ironed just for fun.
I'll spend a fortune at the spa,
Ditch the razor blade;
I'll dye my underarm hair in every rainbow shade!

Forget wearing panty hose,
Let's see how long my leg hair grows;
Call me lazy, call me crazy,
Shaving's not for me;
I'm a dating nightmare,
Hairy as can be!

SMOKED SALMON AND ROE

A little bit naughty,
A little bit nice,
Salty and sexy, decadent spice;
What to do with smoked salmon and roe?
Just bathe me in it, basking in the glow!

Erotic, exotic, they play on my tongue,
Sensuous devils make me feel young;
Exploding fish eggs pop in my mouth,
Eventually swimming on their way south;
Spawning in my stomach walls to live another day,
Winding through intestine tubes,
Just to be flushed away.

All good things come to an end,
Cruel is the truth, my friend;
When Nature calls, there's no control,
Salmon and roe end up in the bowl!

DISTINGUISHED vs EXTINGUISHED

"Distinguished" is a man's white hair,
Salt and pepper, debonair;
"Extinguished" is a woman's curse,
Graying makes it all the worse!

The scales are tipped in favor of men,
Proven time and time again;
When will women have their day,
showing off their heads of gray?

NOISE

6AM .. and so it begins,
I set the alarm to "snooze",
only to wake up to droning voices
on the TV's morning news.

Gardeners are mowing lawns,
those whining hedge trimmers from hell;
Noise! Noise! Noise!
All I crave is my very own padded cell.

Sitting on a park bench, one with nature, alone,
Short-lived bliss, I'm interrupted with a guy yelling on his phone;
Oh where, oh where can I find peace and quiet in this noisy city?
My head is exploding and my patience imploding,
God, it's such a pity.

If I sit on the pot and lock the door,
Do you think they'd leave me be?
Oh no! More noise and frantic knocking ..
I can't even take a pee.

I don't want to listen to loud commercials
or see videos of terrorist violence;
Just give me peace to enjoy
the deafening sound of silence.

VINCENT'S EAR

(The Mystery of Van Gogh's Ear)

If I could hear through Vincent's ear,
What would it say to me?
'Vincent, why did you do it? Couldn't you work through it?
How desperate can you be?'

Did Vincent's ear just disappear?
Was it pickled in a jar?
A brilliant painter, a tortured soul,
Crashed and burned, a shooting star.

"An eye for an eye, a tooth for a tooth",
And then there's "lend me a hand";
Vincent took it literally, we fear,
when he cut you off ..

"LEND ME AN EAR"!

THE NERVOUS KNEE

The nervous knee,
That constant twitch,
Does he have an "on/off" switch?
I'll sit on his jiggling knee,
My God, that guy's annoying me.

Now he's picking up some speed,
I want to slap his face!
He's like the "Energizer Bunny" running in a race.

Amazing he can talk and chew
While tapping on the floor;
I think I'll lose my temper
If I stay one minute more.

Oh no! He switched from left to right,
Talented, I admit;
Pumping pure adrenalin,
Those nervous knees won't quit.

If I stare too long, I know he's bound to put me in a trance;
I'm going to have to straddle him with
one helluva lap dance!

DIRTY OLD MEN

Girls behind the bar, short-shorts
way too skimpy, by far;
Wandering eyes on boobs and thighs,
The more they flirt, the more he buys.

Dirty old men with wallets fat,
Spend the bucks on this and that;
Hours on end, they sit and stare,
catching a glimpse of underwear.

Dirty old men eventually go home
to wives, those "Balls and Chains", never to roam;
Boredom sets in, the daily routine,
'Honey do this, honey do that, mow the lawn,
Help me clean!'

The "Great Escape" is happy hour,
Shave the beard, take a shower;
Leave the wife at home for a while,
Feel young again, wear that smile.

Ogle the girls, take a peek,
Nice to see a young body, sleek;
Youth is wasted on the young, they say,
But dirty old men still like to play.

MARK YOUR BALLS, BOYS

"Fore!" They scatter like ants,
Gaudy shirts, gaudy pants;
Golfers swinging left and right,
Smashing balls with all their might.
A hole-in-one is such a prize,
But it could lead to your demise;
Buying guys a round of booze,
Empties wallets, win or lose.
Mark your balls, boys!
They all look the same;
Dimpled white "Titleists",
Inscribe them with your name.
Balls are flying everywhere,
In underpants and in the air;
One shaft here, one shaft there,
Show 'em all you've got a pair;
NASCAR drivers at the wheel,
Racing to the next hole;
Get it on the green to putt,
Birdie is the goal.
When the scores are tallied,
It's to the 19th's bar;
Each one has a story how he "missed it by that far".
Like tattoos on a body part,
A golf ball is a work of art;
Mark your balls, give it your name,
Those round ball busters look the same!

MUNDANE MONDAY

Poor little mundane Monday,
Nobody loves you, you're the beginning of the week;
Monday Blues, work and worries,
You're the clown, the circus freak.
You're the leftover, the unwanted crumb,
Sunday is a hard act to follow;
Monday is something unappetizing, difficult to swallow.
Tuesday breathes a sigh of relief,
Escaping Monday's stress and grief;
She barely squeaks by, still saving face,
Doesn't mind coming in second
in the week's rat race.
Wednesday is the middle child,
"Hump Day" is her name;
She's half-way home to the weekend,
That's her claim to fame.
Thursday runs the relay race
with her weekend sisters, keeping pace;
Not quite there, she steps aside,
Falling behind fun Friday's stride.
Saturday's playful, parties and fun,
Movies and popcorn,
the beach and the sun.

Sunday is a day of rest,
Laid back, relaxed in her Sunday best;
She's like a soothing bubble bath,
Preparing us for Monday's wrath!

LAYER 4:

ROMANCING THE ROSE

LOVER

Oh, how you weigh on me!
I loved you from the start,
You're the scarlet letter on my heart.

Passion and guilt stroke my conscience
like a gypsy violin;
Why is loving you such a sin?

Lover, your heart is pure,
You're an addiction without a cure;
My pillow's stained with a lover's tears,
Praying I'll wash away my fears.

Lover, come to me tonight,
Kiss me in shadows,
Make it feel right;
Losing ourselves in our private world,
Melting as one;
Reality is an illusion,
A smoking gun.

Fragile is my hungry heart, easily broken in two,
Sacrifice is a hefty price,
I bear the cross for loving you.

SEXY BLUE EYES

Bright blue as the Caribbean,
Serene as the tide;
Moody blue when your skies are dark,
so vulnerable inside.

Sexy when you look at me,
Smokey with desire;
Azul electric, smoldering hot,
As if your soul's on fire.

Sad or teary, I know you're weary,
You have nothing to say;
No words are spoken when your heart is broken,
Your blue eyes give you away.

There is no disguise,
Your heart is true;
Caught up in romance, entwined in our dance,
I love your sexy blue.

I USED TO FEEL

I used to feel the ocean mist on my face,
Now I walk among shadows, feeling out of place.
I used to sing and laugh,
Every day with you I smiled;
Now I'm a lonely outcast,
Abandoned like a homeless child.
I lost you and my world ended,
Extinct as the dinosaur;
I used to have a purpose, now I feel no more.
We made love in the morning,
Soft sunshine kissed your lips;
The sun is hidden behind the moon,
Eternal is my eclipse.
I'm the joke without a punch line,
A story without an end;
I'm the missing piece of a puzzle,
no one to call a friend.
You left me floundering,
a fish dying on the sand;
My screams are lost in a hurricane,
There is no helping hand.
I used to feel love's beauty,
Like a rose, I was adored;
Now I cry desperate tears,
My prayers are ignored.
Dear God, do you hear me?
Will my wounds ever heal?
Please mend my broken heart,
All I want to do is feel.

ONE SUMMER DAY

I took his hand in mine as we walked on the old dirt path,
It was a beautiful warm summer day;
His eyes stared straight ahead of him,
In a trance, he had nothing to say.

I talked of memories, how we met, had a family now grown,
I held the hand of a man I loved,
Yet, feeling so alone.
Now and then he flashed a smile, as if he remembered too,
Only a shell remained of the husband I once knew.

We found a clearing in the woods,
The sun shone through the trees;
I led him to a babbling brook,
He bent down on his knees.
"I remember this place", he laughed with a quivering smile,
"This is where we first kissed, my love. Let's stay here for a while."

For a moment I had him back,
I cherished every word;
His husky voice was the sweetest sound
I think I ever heard.

He laid his head upon my lap
on that beautiful summer day;
With a smile on his face, he closed his eyes,
and quietly passed away.

NO CLAIM, NO BLAME

I'm not here to blame you,
I'm not here to claim you;
I'm just a friend who loves you.

I don't want to tie you down with weighty emotions
or a lover's drama;
There are no rules or curfews,
I don't want to be your mama.

Feel free to cry on my shoulder,
Be naked in your honesty;
When you look into a mirror,
There's only you and me.

I'm just a friend who loves you,
No judgment, guilt or shame;
I'll never try to own you,
There is no claim, no blame.

POISON IN THE WELL

Tainted.   It's all tainted.
It's not a pretty picture by a master painted.
There is poison in the well,
Green is the monster from hell.

Jealousy rears her ugly head,
Like Medusa's snakes of fear and dread;
What used to be so crystal clear
is muddied by deceit and lies;
Laughter and love are now replaced
with our despairing cries.

Don't drink from the cup,
Wine poured from the witch's brew;
Don't eat off the porcelain plate,
She will poison you.

A cancer spreading, a fungus to rot,
She has destroyed
our Camelot.

ALMOND EYES

They were toasted brown, the color of warm caramel.
Her deep almond eyes melted me with one sensual look.

If eyes could hypnotize,
her almond eyes put me in a trance;
I could not pull myself away from her exotic dance.

No words were spoken,
There was no need;
She could make a cold stone bleed.
Her loving gaze said it all,
Deeply in love, I began to fall.

Sparkling like diamonds in a pool of brown,
She pulled me under,
Helpless, I drown.

One look, my heart soared to the skies,
I love your beautiful almond eyes.

THE RICHEST WOMAN IN THE WORLD

I don't need a fancy yacht,
Or diamonds on my hand;
I don't need a million dollars
to make you understand.

You see it in the way I look at you,
With each loving gaze;
You know I'm happy where I am,
I'm yours, always, always.

I have it all right here at home,
No wanderlust,
Don't need to roam;
I'm the richest woman in the world, you see,
I love you,
and you love me.

COME TO YOUR LADY IN DREAMS

He's gone, her love.
Come to her in dreams, restless sleep.

She yearns for your smile, your voice,
Your loving touch.

Just one more time, just one more kiss,
Come to your lady in dreams,
for they are the paths to her reality.

SPONTANEOUS COMBUSTION

You sent tingles through me like an electric shock,
I felt my body begin to rock;
Sucked in like a vortex with a hurricane's might,
Hit by lightning in the night,

I saw you.

Your eyes were whirlpools, dragging me under,
I could not move, then came the thunder;
Standing in your monsoon,
I bathed in the essence of you;
I drenched myself until saturated,
What else could I do?

Helpless, I stood there like a child,
Even the ground shook when you smiled;
The earth moved when you looked at me,
From that moment on,
we were meant to be.

Spontaneous combustion!
We torched the sun,
Danced on the moon, just for fun;
We danced on mountains, swam sea to sea,
You were my love, my destiny.

WHILE YOU CAN

Too many silent moments have passed,
when I could have told you I love you,
or kissed you on the cheek.

Instead, I chose not to speak.

I'll never get those chances back.
They are the ghosts that haunt me when I sleep;
Not finding you next to me,
I begin to weep.

Lost, lost. Those precious smiles and gazes
fade to memories.
Say "I love you", don't wait,
Do it while you can,
Don't hesitate.

As the years slip by, I'm soured and bitter,
I remember when we were young;
Alone, I yearn to see your face again,
I whisper the words I should have said
while you were sleeping in our bed.

I love you, I love you, with all my heart,
even though we are worlds apart;
You were my love,
You were my man,
Grab those fleeting moments now,

Do it while you can.

RAINBOW

A rainbow is a bridge from this world to the next,
A path to the other side;
The colors are the colors of Love and Beauty,
glistening after a storm, a sign of hope, triumphing over sorrow and loss.
That is God's hand, leading us over the rainbow to everlasting peace.

When I lost you, my world crumbled,
Falling to my knees, I was humbled;
Before God, I prayed for Him to take me with you,
My tears fell like a torrent of rain,
shattering my heart in a million pieces.

Red were my swollen eyes, ruby was my rage,
Green was my jealous heart, cold emerald was my gaze;
Longing for you, I watched others in loving embrace,
Yellow was my skin, dry parchment was my face.

Deep blues and purples filled my soul,
I wrapped myself in sorrow,
thinking that I'll never see the sun or a new tomorrow.
The gems piled high upon the ground,
Fragmented colors fell without sound;
Like a knife, diamonds cut deep,
Hard as ice, I could not sleep;
Angels gathered my diamond dust,
Crushed jewels spread across the sky,
They painted my rainbow colors above the gray clouds high;
Brilliant hues sparkled as sunbeams chased the rain,
My spirit soared, my soul was free of all the grief and pain.

Every time I see a rainbow, I know what's at the end;
I'll see you on the other side,
My light, my love, my friend.

TIME WITH YOU

If I had Aladdin's lamp
and was granted a wish or two,
The only thing I'd wish for is
to have more time with you.

The years fly by in the blink of an eye,
Like water through my fingers;
The hour glass empties its grains of sand,
Time never stops or lingers.

I kiss you in the morning as we start another day,
It seems I spend more time at work,
More hours that I'm away.

Our memories are precious,
Each day we start anew;
Please stop the race,
All I want is
to spend more time
with you.

ANCHOR

Chained to the anchor, that old ball 'n chain,
He'll bring me down one day;
He'll drown me with his weighty woes,
Release me, Lord, I pray.

Link by link we forged our life,
Controlling husband, obedient wife;
Swollen ankles, bleeding feet,
The anchor cuts, but be discreet.

Don't ever let the neighbors know,
We keep pretending, all for show;
The house is my prison, reeking of gloom,
Buried alive in my self-made tomb.

One day I'll cut the chains,
Salvage what little remains;
He's the warden, lock and key,
That anchor's going to bury me.

THE LOST ART OF CONVERSATION

Two people together, yet all alone,
Not a word between them,
Each absorbed with their phone.

It was as if she wasn't there,
texting to someone without a care;
She didn't look up, even once in a while,
eyes glued to her IPad, not even a smile.

When did the art of conversation die?
We're too self-absorbed to try;
Why bother to sit face to face at a table,
Ignoring each other for hours?
No wonder a relationship ends with a text,
And love eventually sours.

SEEING THROUGH A BRICK WALL

I wish I was Superman so I could see
All that is secret and hidden from me;
X-Ray vision through concrete walls,
Leaping over Niagara Falls;
Flying warp speed around the world,
But, alas! I'm only human.

How can I penetrate your cold gaze?
Eyes, ice blue, in a foggy haze;
If windows to your soul bare all,
Why can't I see through your brick wall?

One chip at a time, a fortress will crumble,
From your lofty throne, one day you'll tumble;
On your knees you will fall,
Only then will I seen through your brick wall.

IF YOU CAN

If you can say one person loved you in your lifetime,
You've lived a beautiful life.

If you can say that you've helped at least one person
in your lifetime,
You've left a great legacy.

If you can leave this world knowing you've contributed
to its beauty and survival,
You've given the greatest gift of all,

You

BURIED SIX FEET UNDER

All these years confirm my fears,
Did I misbehave, digging my own grave?
This relationship is dying and we're both tired of trying.

We're buried six feet under.

How can we survive if we're buried alive in anger and mistrust?
Who says we need to stay together
like two bookends gathering dust?

A corpse is impossible to revive,
No more alive than your dead eyes staring through me;
Cold silence spreads like a cancer,
as we drown in our sorrowful sea.

Separate beds in two coffins we sleep,
Bitter tears soak my pillow,
I silently weep.

Hear the rain, hear the thunder,
We're buried six feet under.

FROM FRIEND TO FIEND

One small letter, "R", turns a friend into a fiend,
Betrayal, lies, jealousy, hate;
The glass is shattered, the wine is spoiled,
Poison on my dinner plate.

My eyes are clear, but my heart is broken,
Was I so blind to you?
I could not see through your smoke and mirrors,
We loved as one, now split in two.

You became Jekyll and Hyde,
No love remains,
The chasm's too wide.

One little "R" turned a friend into a fiend,
You're the poison on my dinner plate.

DAZE

Staring into the distance, nothing to say,
When did our love fade away?
We sit lost in thought, in our own private daze,
This is our final unhappy phase.

When did we run out of words,
"Hey, honey, how was your day?"
Our sunny skies, once full of hope,
Now weep with clouds of gray.

As cold as tombstones on our graves,
We etched our epitaphs;
Somber, not a smiling face,
No room for loving laughs.

Ghosts of what we used to be,
Now there is no you and me;
Looking through a misty haze,
Staring in our private daze.

ILLICIT LOVE

In the shadows we kiss under cover of night,
In my dreams,
I know you.

There is a fog in your eyes, dreamy, gray,
Like the mist in mine;
Illicit, forbidden,
That is our love.

My fantasy is reality now as I hold your hand;
Shaking, hot sweaty palms burn like our two racing hearts.

Running away to somewhere,
Running away to nowhere.

In my dreams
I always knew you.

WORSHIP

When does love become obsession?

I worshiped him. I worshiped him like a god.
The very ground he walked on was sacred.

The way he looked at me,
The way his voice sounded

He caressed me with every word he spoke,
wrapping me in ecstasy like a comforting cocoon.
Willingly, I walked into his quicksand of desire.

I worshiped him

When the fog lifted, when the magic faded, when he left me,
my world shattered into shards of glass.
Crawling out of his abyss, I saw only a man,
exposed, naked in his deceit.

With clear eyes, I walked away, knowing that the only god I will ever
worship is the one who showed me the light.

Worship.
Love or obsession?

HOLDING HANDS

Not a kiss,
Not a hug,
Just holding hands

That comforting familiar feeling of being loved
without saying a word,

Holding hands

Young lovers, old lovers,
The ones married for all those years,
Still reaching for each other's hand,
as natural as breathing

I will always feel sexy,
Just holding your hand

TEARS

Rivulets of salt stream down my face,
Showing emotion is no disgrace;
Tears flow like a monsoon's storm,
My face is an open wound.

There are tears of joy and tears of sorrow,
Happiness or a doomed tomorrow;
Don't be afraid to let yourself go,
Fragile is the heart you show.

Macho men can break down too,
It's not a sin feeling blue;
I fell in love all over again
with my husband, after all these years;
At a movie, passing tissues,
the two of us shared our tears.
It only shows a caring man,
confident and kind;
An open, honest loving soul isn't easy to find.

I'd rather see the Tin Man cry,
not afraid to rust;
Only a dry uncaring heart disintegrates to dust.

YOU'LL MAKE A HELL OF AN ANGEL

In all the years I've known you,
I didn't see your wings;
I didn't see your halo or other angel things.

Like Alice tumbling blindly down the rabbit hole,
I failed to see your beauty,
Pure faith, pure love, your soul.

As if you were a ghost invisible to me,
I always looked right through you,
How blind could a person be?

Now the sun sets on my horizon,
For the first time in my life,
I reflect on all your kindness,
My angel love, my wife.

I'd love to hold you in my arms,
Kiss you on your cheek;
Tell you I adore you,
Now I cannot speak.

Words are jumbled in my mind,
Emotions choke each breath;
You'll make a hell of an angel,
As in life, so as in death.

PALE BLUE

Pale blue was the sky,
Pale blue was the sea,
A Dali painting, surreal as can be.

Smooth as glass, not a ripple or wave,
Will she take me to a watery grave?

Your heart is cold like the ice in your eyes,
Cold as your words I know are lies;
Pale blue is my mood,
Pale is the day,
Chased by my demons, I sail away.

Haunted by tattered taunting clouds,
Phantoms dressed in ghostly shrouds;
There is no color because of you,

My world is only pale blue,
pale blue

SHE IS LOVE

Love has no boundaries,
No borders, no age;
Love is eternal,
She is a timeless sage.

She's willy nilly,
Sophisticated and silly;
Love is The Smile, The Look,
Tear-stained pages in a well-worn book.

She's holding your hand
walking on sugary sand.

Look behind you ..
She's there,
She is Love

LAYER 5:

OUR HEROES

MY EVERY DAY HERO

He's an every day hero, always there for you,
This is what every day heroes do.

He helps clean the house, tends the yard, and he cooks,
He never gets by on just his good looks!

He's there for the kids, runs the errands and more,
What are every day heroes for?

The every day problems, the big and the small,
On his big shoulders he carries them all.

Never complaining, he trudges along,
Doing his duty, singing his song.

Heart of a lion, courageous, true blue,
This is what every day heroes do.

He doesn't need medals to wear on his chest,
He's loving and kind,
That's what he does best.

He's my every day hero when he walks through that door,
I couldn't be luckier or love him more!

THE THIN BLUE LINE

There is a fine line between good and evil.
I am that fine Thin Blue Line.

I am the Thin Blue Line between chaos and unrest,
Safe harbor in a storm,
This is what I do best.
The beam of light shining in a sea of black
for my brothers and sisters who will never come back.

Like dominoes, if one goes down, so do we all,
Together, united, we're strong;
Order out of anarchy,
Separating right from wrong.

I am the Blue Badge of Courage,
Wearing my heart on my sleeve;
Faith and commitment are what I believe.
Respect those every day heroes you see on the street,
Defenders of law and justice,
No surrender, no defeat.

I am the Thin Blue Line,
Bleeding red, white and blue;
Forever the Watcher,
Forever protecting you.

LAST CALL

For our firefighters who have passed on to a new life.
May God bless you and keep you forever in our hearts.

The bells ring for you.
You do not answer.
It is your Last Call.

The bells chime for the ones we have lost.
Thank you for your service, loyalty and heroism.

"Ring! Ring!"

The bells cut through deafening silence, as we honor you with love
and respect.

"Ring! Ring!"

This is your Last Call.
You do not answer.

WREATHS ACROSS AMERICA
THE CIRCLE OF LOVE

Wreaths in hand across the land,
Remember, Honor, Teach us all to understand.

I walk as a shadow among the graves,
I see my name etched in stone;
Peaceful is my heart,
My spirit soars,
I know I am not alone.

REMEMBER
I sacrificed my life for our freedom.

HONOR
my memory with the wreath of eternal love.

TEACH
our children who will inherit the earth
to cherish our freedom, precious from birth.

Keep our memories alive,
Only then will we prosper and thrive;
Uphold our values and never forget,
"Wreaths Across America",
Respect the Vet.

I walk as a shadow by your side,
Place the wreath on my grave,
I wear it with pride!

CORE

With every beat of my heart,
With every fiber of my being,
To the very core of my soul,
I'm a soldier.

I know no fear but the fear of defeat,
Unshakeable, unbreakable,
I'll fight to the end,
Protecting my country,
never forgetting a friend.

Freedom is never free.
It comes with sacrifice and extreme courage;
I am a son, a husband and a father,
willing to die for my country.

I am the proud eagle flying free,
Just a man, when you look at me;
Look deeper beyond what you see, because

To the very core of my soul,
I'm a soldier.

BEHIND THE FACE

Behind the face riddled with scars,
A hero, survivor of war;
His cane by his chair, a vacant stare,
Fighting in battle no more.

The every day problems are his war now,
The bills pile up unpaid;
Maybe he would have been better off
To die in battle, unafraid.

Medals displayed in a box on a wall,
Memories of how he saved them all;
The bottom line on his decline,
Does anyone care anymore?

STANDSTILL

There is no breeze, no wind blows,
The air hangs like a heavy blanket;
Our flag is at a standstill,
as is the lethargy of Americans.

Where there is indifference,
We truly stand still.

CAMOUFLAGE
(For the women in our Armed Forces)

How proudly she stands in her uniform,
She's a soldier true;
She's a daughter, mom and wife,
Forever protecting you.
Without hesitation, without a second thought,
She knew it was her destiny,
It was the goal she sought.
Look beyond her dusty boots,
Her shouldered weapon ready;
She doesn't question, does her job,
Her hands are strong and steady.
In her moments of solitude,
Thoughts run through her mind;
Memories of family and home,
loved ones left behind.
There is no badge of courage on her sleeve at
end of day,
She doesn't look for lofty praise,
Wouldn't have it any other way.
Stay on the path, stay the course,
She walks the road with no remorse.
Without hesitation, without a second thought,
Our precious freedom cannot be bought;
There is no bargaining, there is no price,
There's only courage and self-sacrifice.
When you see her "camouflaged",
Admire respectfully;
True blue, she wears the stars and stripes,
She's the reason that we're free.

VETERAN

My home is a tin roof, canvas tent,
or maybe a sheet or two;
I don't drive a car or have a pretty home like you.
Once I wore a uniform high on hopes and dreams,
Swore to protect my country,
So long ago, it seems.
Is this what I fought for?
My country let me down;
Lost in a sea of indifference,
I am left to drown.
What happened to the patriots wearing red, white and blue?
Sitting on their marble thrones, promises they spew;
I once wore a uniform, now it's only rags,
Around my neck the medals hang,
along with worn dog tags.
Yes, I was soldier in uniform, wearing it with pride,
Now I hide in shadows, the one you cast aside;
I carried the war on my shoulders with a rifle under my arm,
The souls of your children weighed on me,
protecting them from harm.

You look through me, invisible,
as if I were a ghost;
I'm your conscience,
I'm your veteran,
The one you should love the most.

LAYER 6:

FAMILY AND HOME

WINDY

I named you "Windy" for the winds on the sea,
My dog, my companion,
You're everything to me.

Out on my sailboat, it's only us,
Escaping the everyday problems and fuss;
Your eyes tell me when you're happy or sad,
Your tail's tucked under your legs when you're bad.

You accept me as I am,
Loyal till the end;
But most of all, Windy,
You're my very best friend!

THE KEYS TO HAPPINESS

The key to happiness is to love and be loved,
The circle never ends;
Laugh and be true to each other,
Always surround yourself with good friends.

Never be jealous, there is no room
for doubting love that's true;
Always make time for the little things
in everything you do.

Take one day at a time,
Love will triumph through it all;
No problem is too big to solve,
No favor asked is too small.

Respect your partner's space, just as a seed needs room to
grow;
Love will survive with nurturing care,
You do reap what you sow.

Don't take each other for granted,
Each day is a fleeting ghost;
Be gentle, kind and understanding
To the person you love the most.

MY LITTLE MAN

He's my escort, only six,
My son, my little man;
He tries to match my giant stride,
Keeping up the best he can.

The menu hides his tiny face,
Pretending he can read;
He giggles when I hold his hand,
I'm the apple, he's my seed.

The day he was born
I fell in love with my brand new baby boy;
I felt complete, my miracle,
My tiny bundle of joy!

I know these years are fleeting,
One day he'll be a man;
He'll fall in love, raise a family,
No more my Peter Pan.

For now, I'm happy just being his mom,
I'll cherish every day;
No one can ever take these precious memories away!

DELICATE

So small, so frail,
So delicate is she;
How precious a new baby can be.
A light breeze could carry her away,
sailing with the restless wind at play.

Cradling her in my loving arms,
I'm afraid I'll crush her with a kiss;
I never knew pure love before,
Overwhelming is a moment like this.

Every feature is so tiny and new,
Fresh as day's sweet morning dew;
Delicate is life itself,
She renews my faith in a brand new day,
One look in her eyes and my troubles fade away.

As the budding flowers blossom in spring,
As the baby chicks in nests do sing;
God has a plan for birth and death,
New life, reborn in a baby's breath.

MY DAD

He once was a freckled-face boy,
Running and playing in the sun;
Laughing with the other kids,
A Huck Finn of mischief and fun.

He once was a young man, tall and lean,
Dressed in Navy Blue;
Handsome as he proudly wore
His medals from World War Two.

Pictures from another time, another era past;
Faded photos of his wedding day,
A true love meant to last.

Now stooped with age, he's a wise old man,
His eyes still ocean blue;
Lines etch his face, he earned his place,
With a loving heart so true.

I study him when he's not looking,
Catching glimpses when I can;
He's my hero, He's my dad,
He's the boy inside the man.

THE OLD BLACK LUNCH BOX

Worn with use, years of abuse,
Dad's old black lunch box yawned;
It wasn't pretty, lost its shine,
Not a treasure pawned.
The thermos bottle strapped inside
opened its rusty mouth wide;
Swallowing hot soup to the top,
warming comfort for good ol' pop.
Every morning at 5am, baloney and mayo on bread,
I would have been happy with mom and sis just to stay in bed;
We formed an assembly line in the kitchen,
Bleary-eyed, grumbling and bitchin'.
A Twinkie or a Hostess cake,
Hope dad doesn't get a stomach ache;
Napkins, toothpicks, shut the box,
Don't forget his shoes and socks.
Pressed blue shirt, his mailman's hat,
Jacket on, whew! That's that!
With the lunch box in his hand,
he trudges through the snow;
In early morning's cold winter light,
Back to bed we go.
Dad and "Old Blackie", as years went by,
Carried his lunch box till the day he'd die;
It sits on the shelf, reminder of another day,
Those memories will never fade away;
Soup and sandwich packed inside,
When dad held "Old Blackie" with such pride.

MY MOM

She's the pearl in the oyster, a coveted jewel,
Consoling and wise, she's nobody's fool;
Mom dried all my tears, calmed all my fears,
She always took care of me;
She's a woman, a wife, the giver of life,
My angel she'll always be.

Scraping knees, stings from bees,
Nurse mom gave a hug and a kiss;
A cookie or two made me feel brand new,
These are the things I miss.

The salt of the earth from the day of my birth,
The gold at the rainbow's end;
Irreplaceable treasure, her love beyond measure,
She's my mom,
My very best friend.

GHOST WRITER
(For my mom, Mae)

She writes through me,
I write through her,
She is my ghost writer.

I am the vessel,
She is the cool water flowing like a steady stream;
Behind the veil, thoughts and feelings
reach through the shimmering gauze,
breaking that thin barrier
between two worlds.

Every stroke of my pen is guided by her,
gently, lovingly,
crossing over, touching me, as we become one.

My angel, my mother,
my ghost writer.

ROSES FOR MAMA

Oh, how the red petals melted in swirling warm waters,
Playful with the summer winds blowing
the current toward the waterfall.

Down, down, the petals were carried
over the falls, under the bridge
she so loved.

Mama's ashes kissed the sun,
Dance of life after death,
She was smiling, watching us
loving her with roses.

A SPECIAL SUNDAY

It was a beautiful Sunday
with the kiss of spring in the air,
She wore her floppy blue hat,
covering her thinning red hair.

Just mama and me in the park on that warm, easy day,
She raised her arm to shield the sun from her eyes,
wearing her tinted glasses of rose;
I took her picture as she sat on the bench,
so pretty in her Sunday clothes.

The geese were aggressive, chased us out of the park,
Claiming the lake as their own;
Their noisy quacking made it clear
we're intruders, so leave them alone.

We laughed and held hands, what a glorious day,
The sun felt good on our faces;
The Old Mill Pond with the waterfall
was one of our favorite places.

I still smile through my tears after all these years,
It seems like yesterday;
She's shielding her eyes from the sun, with a smile,
On that beautiful special Sunday.

SARAH'S FIGHT

She was a fighter, a true warrior in life,
Daughter, mother, loving wife;
With every challenge, she faced it with a smile,
Knowing in the end, it was all worthwhile.
She was running out of time,
Days quickly fading away;
Every moment was precious,
Every fleeting day.
Sarah was my best friend,
Loving, spirit free;
We shared so many good times,
So much history.
When she died, I died too,
My world changed from pink to blue;
Heavy is my heart, but I can feel her near,
I see her on a sunny day,
I know that she is here.
She comes to me in dreams,
Free at last from pain;
I know one day, in God's great plan,
We'll be together again.
There is another life, for this is not the end,
I'll laugh and sing with Sarah,
My sister, my best friend.

A THANKSGIVING PRAYER

In times of crisis, in times of sorrow,
There is a new day, a bright tomorrow;
One kind word, one kind act heals a wounded heart,
The Power of Love touches everyone,
This is how we start.

We give thanks for loyal friends,
Bless our families;
Bless our brave men and women fighting overseas.
We've weathered storms, lost loved ones too,
But gray skies always turn to blue.

We gather together on this day,
One with God's great love, we pray;
Protect us from all hate and fear,
Keep us safe, your angels near.

Heaven awaits on the other side,
Pure Light, Pure Love, doors open wide;
The Son of God walks with the living,
Bless us, your children, this Thanksgiving!

I WANT TO LIVE IN MAYBERRY

A small town. Small cares, small worries,
No one's in a rush, nobody hurries.

It isn't a drag race to the light,
There's no violence, no riot, no fight;
This is where I want to be,
In a tiny place called Mayberry.

Andy, Barney, Opie, Aunt Bee,
Come to supper, sip some tea;
Sit on the porch in a rocking chair,
Soak in the night's fresh clean air.

Guitar on my lap, I'll sing an old tune,
Gaze at the stars and the bright full moon;
Yes, that's exactly where I want to be,
Where everyone knows me in Mayberry!

WALKING WITH SOPHIE

I loved to walk with Sophie;
She was tiny and so willing to be my partner,
We walked together, enjoying the day,
just Sophie and me.

We grew old together,
Sharing secrets, quiet times;
Her little legs tried to keep up with my giant stride,
determined to always be by my side.

But time is no friend, and the years put an end
to our old familiar ways;
No more long summer walks, our private talks,
I miss those wonderful days!

Sophie went blind and I tried to find a way to abate her fear;
In her dark world, she cried through the long lonely nights,
But she knew I was always near.

Sophie died in my arms one day,
She's in Heaven, in God's arms, I pray;
Sophie was my dog, you see,
my little girl, my family.

HUMMINGBIRD

I called her "Hummingbird",
My pretty baby girl;
Glittering jewels could not compare,
She was my precious pearl.

As light as a summer breeze,
Annoying like a mosquito's tease;
A little brash, gone in a flash,
Laughter light as a tinkling bell;
Showy, bright, with Vaudeville's flair,
She's the magic coin in a wishing well.

One day my little Hummingbird flew away,
All grown up, tucked in her wings;
no longer Doris Day.

The nights don't shine with soft moonlight,
I miss my Hummingbird's style;
She left her nest like all the rest,
There's no more reason to smile.

Hummingbird,
My pretty little Hummingbird

OLIVIA IN PIGTAILS

She stepped out of a Norman Rockwell painting,
Fresh face, wholesome and clean;
Two pigtails in ribbons,
A star on the Silver Screen.

Innocence of Hepburn,
"Breakfast at Tiffany's",
Could have worn saddle shoes,
sipping ice cream sodas, pretty as you please.

Some day she'll cut her hair in a sassy swinging style,
framing her sparkling eyes and impish girlish smile;
For now, she's my Tinker Bell,
Flying on a magic ship with sails;
I'll always love my freckle face,
Olivia in pigtails!

GRANDPA'S LEATHER BOOTS

If those boots could talk,
If they could walk,
What stories they could tell!
Grandpa's old worn leather boots,
A memory I know well.

Through the years they stuck like glue upon his wandering feet,
Traversing mountains, rain and snow,
Crossing deserts in the heat.
Holes in his soles, frayed laces,
Grandpa wore his boots with pride;
He always kept his trusty book of adventures by his side.

A diary of an explorer, such tales I read with awe,
The tattered cover, worn ink-stained pages
took me places I never saw.
At night he placed those leather boots under his bed with care,
The diary of his life tucked in a knapsack, now threadbare.

Leather boots, worn laces,
Exotic lands, new faces;
Forever a restless spirit may roam,
only to return to family and home.

LAKE'S END

We live at the end of a beautiful lake. That's where everything eventually ends, where the waters flow to a stop, where the grass meets the water, where the tall weeds sprout, right in front of our window.

Carp, those elusive and mysterious fish, spawn flirtatiously, fins in the air, barely visible over the calm water. Except for their sexual splashing, resonating ripples are the only evidence of their existence.

Wading birds test the waters with their webbed feet, feeling for fish, feeding their feathered bellies with gourmet fare of insects, no match for their hungry predators. Occasionally a family of ducks gather for their morning "duckings" underwater. Oh, the conversations going on! If only we could understand their quackings! We are eavesdroppers, spying on their private moments.

The "End" is always the start of new beginnings. She is a moody lake, sometimes low and depressed, shrouded in a foggy cloak. When she's well-fed by a deluge of rain, she's happy and flowing, kissed by sunshine, licking the grassy knolls, teasing with her soft ripples, like dimples in a smile. Ebb and flow, in and out. She's a small sister to her family of oceans, a gathering place for birds feeding, playing, nesting. She provides for her extended family.

"Lake's End" is a mirror, reflecting silhouettes of shimmering rooftops, elusive mountains reaching not to the sky, but the bottom of the lake, just mirages in her watery oasis.

Life begins and ends here, always changing, evolving with every brand new day. New families of hungry babies nest in the trees. What will the lake and land provide for them today? Will Mother Nature, reigning Queen, bend and be generous or will she put on a cold icy face and lay listless and lifeless as a frigid woman?

This is where we live. This is where we will die, by our beautiful Lake's End.

HOME SWEET HOME

A house is made of brick and stone, wooden beams and tile,
It's just a structure, empty until someone makes it smile.
A home becomes a part of every family,
Decorated with loving hands for everyone to see;
White walls are painted, colors flow,
Lights are dimmed for a cozy glow;
Carpets lay where children play,
Curtains closed so you're not exposed.

A home reflects just who you are,
Free to shine like a twinkling star;
It's a refuge, a friendly shelter,
Shutting out all the helter-skelter;
Laughter rings from every rafter,
Love abounds, happiness ever-after.

A man's home is his castle, his own domain,
A safe harbor in a storm;
Shutting out the wind and cold, and always keeps you warm.

As Dorothy said when she clicked her heels,
No matter where you roam,
Be it ever so humble, mi casa su casa,

There is no place like home.

SAFE IN MY ARMS

In Loving Memory of My Mom, Mae
1917-2009

When life gets too tough,
When you've had enough,
You'll always be safe in my arms.

No matter how old you've grown,
With a family of your own,
Remember,
You're safe in my arms.

Wherever you roam,
Just come back home,

Loved
and
Safe in my arms

Mom and Me

ACKNOWLEDGEMENTS

To all my "roses and onions", my family and friends, I thank you for your love and constant encouragement.

A special thanks to Will Lilienthal for his beautiful illustrations. What a talented artist you are, Will!

Thank you to the Cape Canaveral branch of the National League of American Pen Women! Your enthusiasm and passion have inspired me to be a better writer. I am proud to be a member among this group of exceptional women.

Every experience is a layer in life. It can be acidic like the onion or as beautiful as the delicate rose. Revealing our layers one at a time can be terrifying, humbling, inspirational, liberating. Freeing yourself from inhibitions is breaking the chains keeping you from being your true self, standing naked and vulnerable. It truly is exhilarating!

I thank everyone who challenged me to peel back my layers and reveal my inner self. True beauty lies inside all of us.

ABOUT THE BOOK

I would like to point out that my poem, "Wading Through The Waters", won Honorable Mention as one of eight finalists in the 2017 Brevard County Poetry Contest in Florida. I am proud to be in the company of such talented writers and poets!

The poem, "I Want To Live In Mayberry", was sent to the mayor of Mt. Airy, North Carolina. It is now hanging in the Chamber of Commerce, representing "Mayberry" on "The Andy Griffith Show".

"The Thin Blue Line", was written for Sheriff Wayne Ivey, our dedicated Sheriff in Brevard County, Fl. He and all the brave men and women who serve our communities as law enforcement officers should be commended for their loyalty and tireless vigilance. My poem is now framed in Sheriff Ivey's office and it was included in 1,500 Christmas cards sent to the entire department of law officers. I am proud and privileged to have "The Thin Blue Line" representing these wonderful people.

"Last Call", was written as a dedication to our heroic firemen. This framed poem hangs in one of our stations in Viera, Fl. They truly are heroes and we should all be thankful for their dedicated service.

"Wreaths Across America", is dedicated to the wonderful organizations that sponsor this event across America. Wreaths are provided to volunteers who lovingly place a wreath on every veteran's grave. It is a touching memorial to honor our veterans who sacrificed their lives to keep America free. We will never forget!

So many layers, so many inspirations! I am truly blessed to be able to share my writing with all of you.

ROSES AND ONIONS, ONE LAYER AT A TIME

Layer upon layer, we build our lives. Some of us are big as the Rock of Gibraltar, while others are sand pebbles on a beach.

One layer at a time, one experience at a time. This defines who we are. Peel back those layers like an onion and you will expose the true heart of a man, the core of the human psyche.

Admire a rose's beauty. It has infinite layers of delicate spiraling designs. Each petal is unique, like all of us. My poetry has many layers too. Humor, love, wonder, sadness, elation. Like rings on a tree or a single snowflake, not one of us is the same. We make the earth spin. We are all poetry in perpetual motion.

Without the poet, what a dull gray world this would be. From my opening poem, "Layers":

"Freedom is a state of mind,
Let loose the doves to soar;
Breaking through, reborn again,
It's just one layer more."

I have been writing poetry since I was twelve years old. Through my life's experiences, I've continued to write poetry, layer by layer. I grew up in Wisconsin with two sisters, mom and dad. Mom was a poet, author, artist, musician and composer. Through her I developed a love of poetry and dance. Sometimes I blend the two together, which makes for my "dance of words". My writing is from "A to Z", so to speak. Humor, love of nature, raw emotions, personal experiences and the ability to touch anyone who reads my poetry. I live in Melbourne, Florida with my husband, Fred. He is my "muse", my biggest fan. I will always write what is honest and true, which makes my poetry part of every man.

CPSIA information can be obtained
at www.ICGtesting.com
Printed in the USA
BVHW02s0737210718
522243BV00015B/59/P